...From the

Lane...

Oliver Wright

ISBN 978-1-84799-045-7

Preface

Epilogue

Dedicated to the person who somehow made loving an Arsenal supporter possible...

... oh, and to Chris Waddle and Jurgen Klinsmann for providing the inspiration

Preface

I blame it all on Chris Waddle. It is all his fault. I do not hold it against him though. He certainly got me interested in Tottenham in the first place, and I am sure he turned my initial interest into an obsession, an infatuation. Not with him, but with the club. He does not know this, of course. Spurs had plenty of talented players, but it was this mullet-haired winger that caught my eye. Of course, Waddle left Spurs a few years later, and broke my heart for a time one summer, but the damage had been well and truly done by then. The players since (some more than others) must have ensured my relationship with the club continued and strengthened, but it started and was entrenched irreversibly in my being by that man Chris Waddle.

I chose Tottenham Hotspur at the age of eight. Little did I know at the time how joyous, eventful, torturous and emotionally demanding this choice would prove to be. You could say I was foolishly attracted to them as a young boy, but as the years progressed my love for the club developed and I am now irretrievably emotionally attached. The feelings and emotions that this football club bring out in me are akin to those you might experience in any other close relationship. The only difference being that this is a purely one way relationship. I love the club, the players, and they make me happy (or sad), somehow able to control my moods at times. It stands to reason that if something can bring you joy, then it must also have the power to make you sad. The club, however, do not reciprocate my feelings and emotions. Do I personally make the club happy? No. I am one of many thousands who define the football club, but if I were to stop supporting them or leave the country, would the club be affected in any way? No chance. They would do just as well, or badly, without me. If the club were to cease to exist or even if I emigrated would I miss it? Absolutely, more than many things on this earth.

I started supporting Spurs in 1987 and I will do so until either I, the club or football dies. I have been a member of the football club since 1993, being a season ticket holder for the two seasons of 1995/96 and 1996/97. This book charts my first twenty seasons as a supporter of Tottenham Hotspur. I hope the next twenty are more successful than the first; the start of my support seemed to coincide with a decline in the club's fortunes. I have always wondered whether continual success dampens the passion of a supporter. It is something I have never had to worry about and will probably never be able to answer as a Spurs fan; the continual failure to succeed keeps you wanting more all the time. But did the Liverpool fans in the eighties and the Manchester United fans in the nineties feel less passionate about their club when they were winning trophies all the time? I doubt it very much; they just got used to it and wanted it all the more. The difference is that they probably felt disappointment as often as Tottenham feel success.

You have to be an eternal optimist to be a Spurs fan, and indeed a fan of most football clubs, accepting the many disappointments and frustrations that occur in between all the good bits. If, by the time I have finished this book, Spurs have done something extraordinary or won something, in all likelihood it will be a one-off, rather than the start of a period of domination; things will return to their usual inconsistency soon enough. And that is why I am a football fan, waiting for the good bits, however sparse, however fleeting, and enjoying the pleasure of them to the full while they are there. The disappointments only add to the hope and how much you appreciate it when a player scores following a solo run from the edge of his own box, when a 30-yard free kick screams into the top corner at Wembley, when a foreign superstar sets alight a season, when a last minute winner hits the back of the net in a cup final, or when Spurs convincingly beat the opposition against all odds. For me, these are the moments that make supporting and watching Tottenham Hotspur all worthwhile, and more than that, enthralling, exciting and addictive.

As a football supporter, there are some characteristics that people would recognise from my everyday persona. There are other traits, though, that are only evident at a football match, which people who know me may find a little surprising if they saw them. In other words, football can bring out a personality and behaviour in me that is different to that which I show in day to day life. A normally fairly calm, often reserved, person, I become agitated, excitable, sometimes loud and brash when I am watching Tottenham; it may be like being with a different person for some people I know. I do not actually like how it makes me sometimes. Watching Tottenham can change my personality just as much as drink or drugs are able to. An intoxicating atmosphere is just that. You want the win more than anything. For one and a half hours nothing else matters. Half time is a meaningless void, a chance to go to the toilet and get cold. You leave the stadium happy or hurting, rarely in between. You also leave analysing what just happened; well I do in any case. Why did we lose? Where does that draw leave us? What if that incident had been different? What could we have done better? That penalty claim, that shot, that mistake, that referee, that pass. What if? Always endless what ifs. Of course, all the what ifs always add up to a victory that did not materialise.

I do not pretend to be the most die-hard match-goer. In a different life situation I would like to think I would go to many more games than I do and I would still like to have a season ticket in an ideal world. I am not sure, though, whether I would be one of those who would go to Grimsby or Hartlepool on a wet and windy Wednesday evening in the second round of the League Cup. I admire those who do have that commitment, probably at the expense of other things in life, going to the games week-in, week-out, whatever the date or location. Indeed, Tottenham are blessed with amazing levels of support wherever and whenever they play. Nevertheless, I have been to a fair few games, spread over two decades, the vast majority of my life, and every time I am at a match, amongst the crowd, witnessing the action, it is one of my favourite places to be. Passionate and loyal, I want to back the team to the hilt however well or badly they are doing. I love witnessing matches, goals and incidents, which all bring out the fervent in me.

When I am not there, I am always thinking of Spurs when they have a match, watching on television when the match is on, or at least trying to get the result as it happens whatever I am doing. Wherever I am my thoughts are with Spurs at 3pm GMT or BST (or at the variety of other kick off times within the modern television-controlled schedule), willing them to win. When I missed the start of the 2002/03 season because I was away in Thailand, it was imperative for me to check the results of the season so far. The PC screen in the Internet café told me that after four games, Spurs were top of the league with 10 points. I was smiling for the rest of the day. (Needless to say, by the time I had returned home to England, the results had started to deteriorate.)

My heart pounds with nervous excitement when I am watching a game. We were awarded a penalty during a recent televised game; as our striker, Robbie Keane, stepped up to take the kick my heart was beating so hard it felt like it would explode through my chest. I love the electric buzz I feel when Spurs score a goal. It is like no other feeling I have experienced, not necessarily the best feeling a person could experience, but certainly unique. My reaction to a goal going in is a reflex one. I recently described it to a friend who saw me jump up and down, yelling at the screen, in an otherwise quiet pub as being a bit like blinking; I just cannot help it.

I sit among the fans who create the atmosphere and sing the songs. Football without the supporters' atmosphere is not something I would feel so zealously about. For this reason, I often prefer away matches, populated with the loyal and ardent fans, more than the home games. Having said that, I am at home at White Hart Lane. I feel comfortable and content there, and enjoy the camaraderie of being part of a mass of supporters, all different and separate people, but with one vital thing in common for 90 minutes: the overriding will for Tottenham to win.

Why does Tottenham Hotspur bring out all these feelings and exhibit these behaviours in me? Not sure I know. What I know for sure is that they are going to be with me for life, and the reason I have these afflictions is ultimately down to one man: Chris Waddle.

1. I'm Spurs and I know I am

I say I chose to support Spurs because there was no direct reason why I should. I do not support them because of where I come from, as I grew up in the suburbs of south west London, not north London. Neither do I support them because of any family history of supporting the club. My Dad used to support Chelsea before he turned his allegiance not only away from them, but from football altogether, and onto rugby. I started being taken to see the oval-ball game from an early age, and certainly before I attended my first football match. Even though I enjoyed these Saturday afternoons out, and still have an affection for rugby, much of my time was spent kicking a football around on the reserve pitches at then-amateur rugby clubs all over London.

My first real memory of watching football was the 1986 FA Cup Final, when Liverpool beat Everton 3-1. I remember lining up my Panini sticker swaps of the two teams in front of the television to help identify the players. I wanted Everton to win on the day and I suppose I supported them that afternoon. I do not recall being particularly affected by "my team's" loss that day though. The 1986 World Cup in Mexico passed by that summer, and my interest in football, and a certain Gary Lineker, grew. Although England were eliminated by the hand of Diego Maradona, Lineker was the tournament's top scorer with six goals.

The Tottenham team of the 1986/87 season is probably still the best of my Spurs-supporting life. That season was certainly more successful than any since: a top three finish in the league, FA Cup runners-up and a semi final appearance in the League Cup. A mixture of this imminent success and the many flair players, including Waddle, was probably the reason Spurs came to my attention. I presume at the back of my mind was the fact that they were a London team and so my chances of seeing them play were significantly higher than, for example, Everton. Clive Allen scored an amazing 49 goals that season, and I used to run around the garden at home, pretending to be Waddle crossing the ball for him to crack the ball into the net. I was in fact ruining some very edible raspberries if I recall correctly. Saturday 25th 1987 was the day my irreversible choice of following Tottenham Hotspur really started though.

I was eight years old when I first went to White Hart Lane, and so for the first few seasons of supporting them I had to rely on being taken. I knew no one else who supported them, so that route to the Lane was closed. The obvious candidate for my chaperone was my Dad. Unfortunately, though, each of his Saturday afternoons was taken up watching London's rugby teams, and Wasps in particular. This meant the first few games I went to see had to be scheduled around this, and so they were either towards the beginning or end of a season, with the odd midweek game thrown in.

As excited children do at Christmas, I awoke very early on the morning of the first game I was to go to. Obviously, as at Christmas, I had to wake my parents up to share in my excitement at the prospect of seeing Waddle, Hoddle and company. Spurs were playing Oxford United, who have since drifted down the leagues considerably. My Dad had got us tickets in the West Stand upper tier, at a cost of eleven pounds each. The price of these exact seats in 2007 is now around five times that amount. They were, from a viewing perspective, the best seats in the house. I do not know why but I cannot really remember much about the game that day. Maybe I was in awe and it was too much to take in – the atmosphere, the stadium, the superstar players, not to mention the actual game. Most of my memories from the game came from subsequent video highlights. The match was selected for a video called Greavsie's 6 of the best from the 80s. It was obviously a memorable game; if only I could have appreciated that on the day.

Something that sticks in the mind, however, is the announcement as the players enter the pitch. "Welcome to White Hart Lane, the world famous home of the Spurs" sounds around the stadium before every home game. This time, though, they were welcoming me for the first time and I felt privileged.

The Spurs team that day was as follows: the reliable England international Ray Clemence was in goal; there was a solid defence with Chris Hughton and Mitchell Thomas on the flanks and Richard Gough and Gary Mabbutt in the centre. Then, there was the wonderfully creative midfield of Steve Hodge, Ossie Ardiles, Paul Allen, Glenn Hoddle and Chris Waddle, and we were spearheaded by Clive Allen up front. Combined, these players made a wonderful team and I can see why I was attracted to them. They were not quite the best team in

15

the country, but they were widely acknowledged as the most attractive to watch.

Spurs won 3-1 thanks to goals from Paul Allen, Chris Waddle and Glenn Hoddle. A young Dean Saunders scored for Oxford in between the second and third Spurs goals. It was Hoddle's last goal for Spurs, and I feel privileged to have been there for that goal – it is still shown on the big television screens at the ground before matches. The ball was headed out of the Spurs penalty area and found Hoddle half way inside his own half with most of the Oxford players pushed up looking for an equalising goal. Hoddle ran at the remaining two Oxford defenders who were stood on the half-way line, rounded them both in one easy motion, before advancing and dummying the goalkeeper, rounding him and rolling the ball into the empty net. It was a truly magical goal, made to look far easier than it was. The game would have been over much earlier than when Hoddle scored with five minutes to go had either of his or Waddle's exquisite chips from 25 yards dipped in rather than clipping the crossbar. A few minutes after Hoddle's goal the final whistle sounded, followed by "Glory, Glory Tottenham Hotspur" ringing around the stands.

For whatever reason, whether it was the game, players, stadium, atmosphere or a mixture of all these, I was hooked and could not wait to get back to the Lane as soon as possible. Unfortunately, the summer was in the way of a swift return.

As I have said, the 1986/87 season was Tottenham's most successful since I started supporting them. Spurs finished third in the First Division and reached the semi final of the League Cup, where the tannoy announcer famously tempted fate by announcing ticket details for the final at half time in the second leg when Spurs were leading 2-0 on aggregate against Arsenal. Arsenal needed no further incentive. In the FA Cup Final, Coventry City beat Spurs 3-2 in front of 98,000 at Wembley in one of the most recent truly great finals, and so I watched my team losing the match for the second year running, except this time I felt the defeat. The end of the season also saw Glenn Hoddle expectedly leave Spurs for Monaco, after many years of being Tottenham's lynchpin.

I have seen Spurs play Chelsea more times than any other team, including at the next game I attended, soon after the start of the following season. August 22nd 1987 was, until very recently, the only time we had beaten Chelsea at home in the league since I started supporting the club. Nico Claesen scored the only goal with five minutes remaining. This time we were sat only a few rows from the pitch in the West Stand lower tier. I remember my sense of awe at how close the players were, and the sound of the ball against their boots and on the grass and the shouts from player to player. Looking back it was probably this day that my unwavering obsession with Chris Waddle began. It was only until researching for this book recently that I was sure it was Waddle who had scored the goal that day. Only after consulting the record books have I realised that Waddle in fact crossed the ball for Claesen. I only saw Waddle play a handful of times in his career, but he was my schoolboy hero for years.

As a child, football is all about heroes, players you want to be like, players you want to score every week and players you imagine being when you play football at school or down the park. For some reason, I always wanted the top players to score in the games I saw live or on television. It seemed that the goal meant more if scored by the likes of

Waddle or Clive Allen, rather than a defender or first team fringe player.

I used to try and copy Waddle down the right wing. A teacher once advised me I should try to cut in sometimes instead of going on the outside all the time; the immediate reaction in my head was that Chris Waddle usually went down the outside and it worked for him. As I write this now in my mid-twenties, those boyhood heroes are long gone. For a start, most of the players I go to support at Tottenham are younger than me. You still have favourites, players that excite and are committed, but no heroes as such. If anything, I find myself having aspirational heroes now, players you wish you could have been in another life but know there was no chance of that ever happening. Also, as you gradually realise, as a child, that players come and go, your attachment to the club itself, rather than the players, strengthens.

Initially, my following of Spurs was, apart from actually attending a very few matches, limited to checking the results in the newspapers and seeing the odd live match on television. I was beginning to think that whenever I actually went to a game, Spurs would win. If I was there they could not possibly lose. Two more games, against West Ham and then Watford four days later, in the hectic Christmas and New Year period resulted in two more wins. They both ended 2-1. I can remember nothing about these two matches, nothing at all. I could not name the scorers or anything that happened on either day. Maybe they were forgettable games, as many are, or maybe I was still caught up in the whole occasion of seeing my team play in the flesh at White Hart Lane. Maybe I was just too young to remember.

My illusions of remaining unbeaten as a supporter were shattered spectacularly when, the following month, I was treated to a family trip to my first evening match. As part of the deal that took Hoddle to Monaco, the two sides played a friendly match at White Hart Lane. Looking forward to this all day at school, the plan was to arrive early and visit the club shop to buy the current home shirt as a birthday present, followed by watching Spurs win again. Unfortunately, due to reasons I cannot remember, which were likely to be the trains (either that or my Dad being late), we arrived at the ground only just in time for kick off with no time to visit the shop. A little upset, I was soon cheered up by the knowledge that the shirt could be bought at the next game or through mail order and, vitally, by the thought of watching my team play.

That evening was my first experience of a magical feeling that still gets me every time it happens. At evening games, as you emerge into the stadium after climbing the steps from the dark area beneath the stand, you are greeted by the special sight of the floodlit stadium. The night sky above you glows and the pitch shines under the light. The surroundings draw you in even more than usual, possibly as it feels as though there is nothing outside this illuminated area, certainly nothing important. Much to my great disappointment, Spurs could not further the magical experience that night, losing comprehensively 4-0, with Hoddle scoring twice. The long journey home to south west London was a depressing one, and the night ended with me in tears in my bed, a birthday seemingly ruined. Surely just a childish reaction; you would never see grown men crying over football, would you?

At the end of the season, I got my first taste of Wembley. A friend invited me to the Sherpa Van Trophy final, a competition for the lower league clubs, between Wolves and Burnley. The game itself held no real interest for me, but I remember being a little in wonder at the size and history of Wembley. I hoped to return one day to see Tottenham play there; unfortunately this would not be for some time.

The close season saw Tottenham sign Paul Gascoigne for £2.2 million, breaking the British transfer record in the process. In the modern football climate, it is a distant memory, Spurs being able to break the transfer record and offer the highest wages, tempting the hottest prospect in English football to come to White Hart Lane, spurning the advances of Alex Ferguson at Manchester United.

Some people might say that as a supporter of Spurs you should be used to crying. Nevertheless, I did not expect to be in tears again at the next match I was taken to. It was another evening game in the November of the season following the Monaco disaster. My father was never early for an appointment, and rarely on time, but given how upset I had been at arriving only just in time for kick off at our previous match, being late should have been avoided at all costs. After traversing the usually busy north circular, we were a little tight on time. I was not unduly worried, though, as we just had to park up and walk to the ground.

Twenty minutes into the game, we were stuck in a traffic jam in a quiet residential road. Like us, many cars were trying to find somewhere to park and there was such an overload of vehicles from both directions that we were stationary for at least a quarter of an hour. Sensing my unrest, my Dad even enquired with a member of the local constabulary how much the fine would be if he left the car on some double yellows. The price, and the prospect of clamping, did not, understandably, persuade my father to leave the car where it was. After eventually finding somewhere to park and a slow run to the stadium, we finally took our seats half an hour into the game. This is not the ideal scenario for a boy who probably looked forward to going to Tottenham matches more than anything else. My misery was compounded when the electronic scoreboard told me I had missed what turned out to be Tottenham's only goal of the night. I did get to witness Coventry City's equaliser though.

I attended one other game that season, a 2-1 win against Norwich City in February. This was Chris Waddle's final season at Spurs, and he left a sense of what could have been behind him. He chose to save his best to last, and justified the £4.5 million transfer fee paid by Marseille with a series of quite outstanding and outrageous goals. The only similar scoring streak I can think to compare this to was when Le Tissier was at the top of his game and scored half the candidates for goal of the season one year in the mid-1990s. Waddle scored one of his collection of spectacular goals that year in the Norwich game. A trademark jinking run down the wing ended with a shot from about 15 yards out; the extraordinary thing was he was also only about two yards from the by-line.

My following of Chris Waddle extended beyond his time at Spurs. This is the only time I have had any real (positive) feelings towards, or support of, a player after he had left the club. The following season I bought the Marseille shirt and Sheffield Wednesday almost became a second club to me when he returned to England a few years later. After winning three consecutive French League titles in a star-studded Marseille team, of which he was an integral part, Waddle continued his form in England as he had left off at Spurs and was voted the Football Writers' Footballer of the Year while at Wednesday.

Unfortunately, Tottenham were not good enough to provide any honours to Waddle, and so when Arsenal and Sheffield Wednesday contested both the League Cup and FA Cup finals in 1993, I was supporting Wednesday and Waddle even more vigorously than I might have supported any other team against Arsenal in a cup final. Arsenal won the League Cup, which surely left a fairy tale FA Cup win on the horizon for Waddle. A draw in the first game meant a replay. Waddle scored an equaliser in the second half, causing me such a shriek and thud of feet on the floor that my mother thought I had seriously damaged myself in the living room. Alas, Waddle was denied his FA Cup win by a last minute Arsenal winning goal. The Wednesday players, Waddle included, were devastated. So was I, for him I think.

In April 1989, I was taken to my first England game at Wembley. It was against Albania in a World Cup qualifier. England ran out 5-0 winners, a young Gascoigne characteristically scoring the fifth and best goal of the night, after dribbling round a couple of defenders. It was my first taste of live international football, but I was not overwhelmed. Club football was my passion, and I will always support club over country. I enjoyed going to see England play and going to Wembley was special, but given the choice I would rather watch Tottenham every time.

Gary Lineker arrived in the summer of 1989 from Barcelona, to link up with Gascoigne and, if only he had stayed, Waddle. Spurs were to finish 3rd that season, without Waddle, and I honestly believe that had he stayed and played anywhere near as well as he had the previous season, Spurs could have won the League that year. With Gascoigne orchestrating things in midfield, Waddle roaming imperiously down the wings and Lineker the goalscorer supreme spearheading the attack, Tottenham Hotspur would have been a match for anyone. One thing is for sure: they certainly have not had a team since capable of reaching anywhere near that standard.

I knew what an exciting signing Lineker was: I had seen what an excellent striker he was for Everton and in the 1986 World Cup for England. I was desperate to get to see him in action after he joined Tottenham. Luckily for me, Lineker scored all three goals in the only Spurs match I saw that season, a 3-2 win at home to Queens Park Rangers. It was the first hatrick I had seen by any player. It was a special day for me as a child, and I relished it even more, expecting as I did that it was likely to be the only time I saw Spurs that season.

My Dad had started taking me to the odd Chelsea or Brentford game, both clubs being much nearer to our home in south west London. Although I still enjoyed going to watch professional football, I did not have a real preference either way who won. I would want Brentford to beat their opponents, but at the end of the game I was not happy if they had won or sad if they had lost. None of my heroes were playing either. It just was not the same if Spurs were not there but it was better than nothing.

I did actually see Spurs one other time that season, but it was not the Spurs I knew. In a charity match at St. Albans, a team of Spurs and Arsenal stars from the past played a team of International Allstars, whose team included such legends of the game as Bobby Moore, George Best, Franz Beckenbauer and Geoff Hurst. I was too young at the time to really appreciate the significance of the players, but I still have the programme today, autographed by all these illustrious stars. I really did see an awesome collection of players that day. For the record, the Spurs and Arsenal team won 6-5, a score reflected by the lack of importance of the actual result and, more likely, by the age of the players.

At the end of the 1989/90 season came the World Cup in Italy. As a birthday present, I had been to a warm-up friendly against Brazil at Wembley a few months previously, Gary Lineker scoring the only goal of the game. With the Spurs stars Lineker and Gascoigne, and my hero Chris Waddle, all in the squad that summer, I was excited about seeing how they would perform for the national team. There was, of course, also the blind hope that spreads across the nation before every World Cup and European Championship that England might actually win the tournament for the first time since 1966.

As it turned out, the 1990 tournament remains the most memorable for England since that 1966 triumph. It was a World Cup famed for Gazza's tears and theme-tuned by Pavarotti's Nessun Dorma, a truly great anthem to get the football emotions flowing. With some fairly uninspired displays in the group stages, England managed to qualify for the knock-out rounds. Then, a goal in the 119th minute, a David Platt volley from Gascoigne's pass, against Belgium put England through to the quarter finals, where England went on to beat Cameroon 3-2, with Lineker netting twice. A semi final against the old enemy West Germany was waiting.

By the time the semi final came around I had gone on a school trip to northern France. The teachers decided we could all watch the game. Unfortunately, my room mate, obviously looking for a way to pass the time, decided to throw objects out of our hotel window into the open windows of other rooms. Understandably, someone objected to this and he worked out roughly where the projectiles were coming from and, being a teacher of another school, came to report it to our teacher. The punishment was obvious: we were not to be allowed to watch the game, soon to kick off, and instead we were grounded in our room. It would be somewhat of an understatement to say I was not very happy with my room mate.

The result was written up on a board at breakfast the next morning, when I learned the tragic news. It was not until I returned home and watched the whole match on video that I appreciated what an occasion it had been. England were the better team that night, and could well have gone on to beat Argentina in the final, if only they could have had a bit of luck against West Germany. A huge looping deflection off Paul Parker, putting the ball in about the only area of the goal Peter Shilton could not reach, put the Germans 1-0 up. With 10 minutes of normal time remaining, Lineker popped up to finish clinically and bring the game level. So the score remained until it was time for penalties. Everybody remembers the penalties missed by Stuart Pearce and Chris Waddle, the latter especially as it was his miss that ultimately gave West Germany the win. What is often forgotten in accounts about this match is that Waddle twice very nearly won the game for England with two attempts worthy of winning any match. First, a low powerful shot from 25 yards came back off the middle of the post, and then he hit the crossbar from about 45 yards out with a chip that would have been one of the greatest World Cup goals ever had it dipped in. These two near misses were reminiscent of the type of goals he had been scoring regularly in his final season at Spurs. Alas, for him and for England neither of them hit the back of the net.

England had done well though, better than most had realistically thought. They were greeted back in England by thousands of fans and a fanfare as if they had been triumphant. In many ways, they had too. Lineker had cemented his hero status, and Gazza had emerged as a star on the world stage, something that Spurs fans had already seen evidence of.

The first Saturday of the season is always one of my favourite days of the year. After the summer break with no club football, there is a chance to see any new signings and every team starts on the same level again. There is nine months of football to look forward to. Most importantly, fans have been allowed to build up unrealistic hope for the forthcoming campaign. If we can just get off to a flying start this year, maybe we can maintain it for the whole season and win the League. As a Tottenham fan, this is unrealistic certainly, but hope is a football fan's greatest weapon.

In the first home game of the 1990/91 season, both Lineker and Gascoigne were greeted by a standing ovation back at White Hart Lane. They had done the country and club proud. My Dad took me to the game, again my only one that season. It was my first Spurs match that I had stood at. We were on the terraces in the East Stand, and I felt as though I was one of the proper fans at last. My Dad obviously thought I was now old enough to stand safely and so we did not have to sit on the expensive seats. We got to the ground very early to ensure that I, as a short boy for my age, would be able to get to the front and see the game. It was one of the few times I stood on the terraces, as not long after that season they had to be replaced with seats in the wake of the Hillsborough tragedy.

There was a party atmosphere that day, in celebration of England's two returning heroes. It was a warm, sunny afternoon and there was a lot of colour in the terraces behind the goals. The party intensified as Spurs worked their way to a 3-1 victory. Fittingly, Lineker scored twice, and Gascoigne the third, to cap off a fine day. It was the start of a special season for Spurs and for Gascoigne in particular. He would make a name for himself in more ways than one.

2. Is Gascoigne going to have a crack?

"Is Gascoigne going to have a crack? He is you know.... Oh I say! Brilliant! That is schoolboy's own stuff.... Ohhh I bet even he can't believe it.... Is there anything left from this man to surprise us? That was one of the finest free kicks this stadium has ever seen."

Barry Davies, 14th April 1991

FA Cup semi final, Tottenham Hotspur v Arsenal

His intent filled run-up signalled that there was not any doubt in Paul Gascoigne's mind that he was going to have a crack at David Seaman's goal. The result was one of the most significant goals in the history of Tottenham Hotspur, and one of the best under the twin towers. To be etched in the memory forever. This FA Cup semi final is one of the two Spurs matches that I did not go to but wished I could have more than any other. The second of these matches is an FA Cup quarter final away at Liverpool in 1995.

The thing that I remember almost as much as the goal itself is the image of the fans as Gascoigne runs towards them and then jumps, fists clenched. The television and video images show a fluid mess of delirious Spurs fans, bouncing and jumping around, shouting with euphoria. I try to imagine being there, among all this. It was such an important moment in Tottenham's, and football's, history: five minutes into the first FA Cup semi final at Wembley, the first semi final played between Arsenal and Spurs, Gascoigne, the golden boy of English football, Spurs playing the champions elect. Add to all this the tradition of Spurs in the FA Cup, and the fact that this was the chance to return to Wembley in the FA Cup final. It is five minutes in, there is an electric, but distinctly nervous, atmosphere floating around the stadium, and Tottenham's good start to the game results in a free kick 30 yards out. You knew Gascoigne would have a go; this could be the greatest start possible. It was and there is an explosion of noise and movement around the blue and white half of Wembley.

I love watching the reaction of supporters at key moments in football matches, the image of them erupting as a winning goal hits the back of the net in the last minute, the image of supporters at the other end of the stadium distraught at that same goal. Every incident in a match affects supporters in different ways and I, as a supporter, enjoy watching what that goal on the pitch has done to the fans off it, either in the ground or on television, because you understand how they feel. I want the camera to pan to the supporters to see what they are doing, how they have reacted.

One particular moment sticks in the mind regarding the emotions of football fans. In 1995, Blackburn Rovers won the League, just. It went down to the last day of the season between them and Manchester United. United had to get a win at West Ham and hope that Blackburn drew or lost at Liverpool. If Blackburn won at Anfield, they would win the League regardless. Every fan of the two teams must have been watching one game and listening to the other. As both games went into injury time at the end of 90 minutes, both were level. As United were bombarding the West Ham goal, Jamie Redknapp scored a free kick to put Liverpool 2-1 up. The looks on the faces of the Blackburn fans were of utter disbelief and sheer sadness. Suddenly, the crowd got news of full time at Upton Park and the sadness turned to unbridled joy as they realised that they had in fact won the League. It showed the extremes of the feelings you can experience as a football fan, all within a five-second period. The Blackburn players were jumping around on the pitch, being congratulated by Liverpool players, even though their game had not quite finished.

Rather annoyingly, in my life as a fan, one of the greatest experiences as a football supporter must have been as an Arsenal fan in the Anfield Road end in May 1989. The final game of the league season was between the top two sides in the division, Liverpool and Arsenal. The only way Arsenal could win the championship was to win the match by two or more goals, an unlikely feat given Liverpool's home advantage and influence of the famous Kop. It was looking that way, too, for much of the match. Even when Alan Smith put Arsenal 1-0 up everyone expected Liverpool to hold out. No-one beat them 2-0 at Anfield. Then, in the dying minutes, just as all Arsenal fans must have resigned themselves to the fact that although they had put up a good fight the League title was staying at Anfield, Michael Thomas latched onto a loose ball and was through on goal with only the goalkeeper, Bruce Grobbelaar, to beat. "It's up for grabs now" cried Brian Moore, surely one of the best timed and greatest pieces of football commentary ever uttered. Every single heart behind that Anfield Road goal must have stopped momentarily. Thomas lifted the ball over Grobbelaar into the net. Cue bedlam on the terrace. It is the ideal scenario for a football fan. Against all odds, last minute goal, right in front of you, to win the championship. I do not mind saying I am jealous of each and every Arsenal fan who was there that night.

Anyway, back to beating Arsenal, rather than lingering too long on one of their greatest nights. The players and fans had only just calmed down after that Gascoigne masterpiece when a good move down the right led to the ball dropping five yards out for Gary Lineker to poke the ball into the net. The Spurs fans could not believe this. They were 2-0 up after ten minutes against Arsenal in an FA Cup semi final at Wembley. It was like a dream. Alan Smith pulled one back for the Gunners just before half time and they pressed hard for an equaliser in the second half. Then, with 75 minutes gone, Lineker received the ball in the centre circle and advanced forward. Vinny Samways made a diagonal run and Lineker "used him by not using him", as Barry Davies described it, moving into the space created. He skipped past Adams and hit a weak left foot shot at the perfect height for a goalkeeper to save. Wonderfully, though, it slipped through David Seaman's fingers and went into the far corner. Lineker was left rejoicing on the ground, possibly recovering from his longest-ever dribble. It was 3-1 and the stuffing had been knocked out of Arsenal. It was Tottenham's day. In all honesty, we outplayed Arsenal that afternoon. Tottenham's lovely passing game coupled with pieces of luck at both ends meant that we won the match quite comfortably in the end.

Gascoigne was running around the pitch at the final whistle like an over-excited schoolboy. Despite a distinctly average league campaign, Spurs had been single-handedly taken to the FA Cup final by Paul Gascoigne. He scored some great goals on the way. The semi final day turned out to be the greatest of Gascoigne's career, although he may disagree. He was off to get his suit measured.

The 1991 FA Cup final was unfortunately shaped by many bad decisions, from players and officials alike. First Gascoigne decided he would try to remove Gary Charles's kneecap instead of trying to get the ball; the referee should have at least booked Gascoigne by this point, if not sent him off; then the referee missed Lee Glover bundling Gary Mabbutt off the end of the wall so that Stuart Pearce could curl the ball into the top corner for the opening goal; the linesman then wrongly flagged for offside and the referee disallowed the goal Gary Lineker had just scored; Lineker then chose to put the ball just where Mark Crossley could save it from a penalty kick; and ultimately Des Walker put his head to the ball and sent it into the top corner of the net, scoring the own goal that won Spurs the Cup.

I watched the game, and all the build up, on the television in my parents' bedroom, as I did the semi final. I was encamped up there all afternoon, eventually emerging at the end of extra time with a massive grin on my face. Gascoigne was overly hyperactive in the final, after which he was never the same player again. Many people speculate that had he joined Manchester United, under the watchful eye of Alex Ferguson, instead of Spurs, he would have continued his advance to becoming the best footballer in the world. The FA Cup Final in 1991 turned out to be his swansong in many ways.

It is rather strange when I think about it now, but I remember feeling a slight discomfort at the time that Spurs had won the Cup because of an own goal. I thought how I would much rather a Spurs player had put the ball in the net; the win would then have been more proper somehow.

Despite winning the Cup, Terry Venables was not in charge for the start of the next season. As a twelve year-old boy, I did not really understand what was going on at the time. All I knew was that Venables had been part of Alan Sugar's takeover of the club and had taken a position in the boardroom rather than in the dugout. Peter Shreeves was appointed as manager for the 1991/92 season. It did not quite work out for Venables, as over the next couple of years the Spurs hero developed some kind of power struggle with chairman Sugar. Venables was sacked in 1993 and the whole affair ended up in court. Spurs fans backed Venables all the way, but he was eventually found not to be quite the innocent party Spurs fans thought he was.

My Dad took me to two games that season, both early on. On our family holidays, always in some part of France, I would come armed with the fixture list and then try to get my Dad to agree to which games he would take me before the rugby season started. I would not let up until I knew at least what the first game I was going to see would be.

That season it was against Chelsea in August, probably more than anything else because my Dad wanted to see his old team. My younger brother, Simon, came to the game as well and I have some photos of me next to him dressed in the Spurs kit I had made him wear. (He is a Liverpool supporter.) The game was to prove to be the first competitive game I had seen Spurs lose. Typically it would have to be against Chelsea, just to set the scene for the coming years. To be honest, I had been incredibly lucky up to that point with the games I had seen: in eight league games, I had witnessed seven wins and a draw, a winning ratio I could only dream of Spurs having all through a season.

In truth, Chelsea ran away with game at a time when they often occupied the lower reaches of the league. They went 3-0 ahead. Kerry Dixon scored the first as our goalkeeper Erik Thorsvedt allowed his header to creep through his hands and Kevin Wilson added the second by lobbing Thorsvedt who was then inexplicably about 25 yards from his goal. Andy Townsend added a third in the second half. Gary Lineker scored a consolation that was not even that. I was despondent. I did not see enough games a year to afford a comprehensive loss like this.

The FA Cup success of the previous season meant we were playing in the European Cup Winners Cup. Spurs were competing in their first European campaign since the ban on English clubs was lifted. My Dad took me to see my first (and only for many years) European game, against unknown Sparkasse Stockerau, a couple of weeks after the Chelsea debacle. Unusually, we stood on the sparsely filled Park Lane terrace behind the goal; we normally sat on one of the sides of the pitch.

I am obviously aware of the club's great European tradition and the historic "Glory Glory Nights". It was all before my time and, while I can appreciate the history, Tottenham have hardly been in European competition in all the time I have been supporting them, which rather reflects our lack of success in the domestic competitions during this time.

I remember very little about the match. There seemed to be a lot of sideways passing and the game was slower, probably a reflection of the competition and opponents. Gary Mabbutt scored the only goal of the game with a less than powerful shot from the edge of the box at the far end of the ground from where I was stood. I remember thinking it was not a great view; little did I know behind the goal was the place I would choose to sit every week a few years down the line. I did not appreciate fully the importance of the atmosphere at a match when I was twelve; I just wanted to see the game,

Although Tottenham reached the semi final of the League Cup, where Nottingham Forest gained revenge for the FA Cup final defeat, it was not a great season for the club. We finished a lowly fifteenth in the league and got dumped out of the FA Cup at the third round stage for the third time in four years, this time by Aston Villa.

Peter Shreeves was replaced after just one season in charge by the duo of Doug Livermore and Ray Clemence for the 1992/93 campaign. The season marked the start of the Premiership, which has since ensured the rich got richer and the poor got poorer. It is no coincidence that the top division has been dominated by a select band of clubs since the Premiership's advent. Few clubs have infiltrated the top four. In the old First Division, while there would be the dominating forces of the time, a wider range of, often smaller, clubs could and did finish in the top few places through the 1980s. It is now quite an achievement to finish fourth in the Premiership.

That season also saw the current back pass rule introduced, whereby goalkeepers could no longer pick up the ball from a deliberate pass from a member of their own team. It resulted in several comical episodes as goalkeepers and defenders slowly adapted to the idea. The 'keepers were not used to kicking under pressure and often miss-kicked. Sometimes they just forgot about the new rule and picked up the ball. The referees seemed unsure of technicalities too. Should the free kick be taken from where the back pass was made or where the goalkeeper picked it up?

There was one such incident in the only league game I went to that season, at home to Everton. One of our defenders passed a simple ball back to our goalkeeper Ian Walker, expecting him to clear the ball upfield. Walker just picked it up, seemingly oblivious to the new rule. The referee then incorrectly gave the free kick from where the defender had passed it, instead of where had Walker picked it up. It was a favourable decision for Spurs as the free kick was taken on the edge of the box, instead of about eight yards out as it should have been. Incidents like that were happening all over the country.

Spurs ran out 2-1 winners that day thanks to goals from Paul Allen and a late winner in injury time from Andy Turner, a teenage midfielder who, after a couple of seasons in the first team squad, never quite made it.

A short while into the season Teddy Sheringham joined the club from Nottingham Forest for £2.1 million. He was a big name signing for the club and the man to replace Gary Lineker as our star striker. (Lineker had left in the summer to finish his career in Japan.) It was a lot to live up to at a club like Spurs and he did not settle in straight away, looking nervous in front of goal. He soon found his feet, however, and the chant "Oh Gary, Gary ..." was quickly replaced by "Oh Teddy, Teddy ...". He proved himself to be a more than adequate replacement and finished the season as the league's top scorer with 22 goals, with a further 7 scored in the cups.

I had the chance to see Sheringham play soon after he joined. Spurs had drawn my local team Brentford in the second round of the League Cup, and my Dad took me along to Griffin Park to stand with the home fans. It was my first away game, although it did not really count as I was not in the Tottenham end. As expected, Spurs won easily 4-2 on the night and 7-3 on aggregate. I was delighted to see Sheringham score twice; Anderton and Turner added the others in an entertaining game.

I was stood right behind the team dugouts and it was exciting being so close to some of the Spurs players. They were virtually within touching distance.

That season Spurs reached the FA Cup semi final again. We were playing Arsenal once more at Wembley. Could we repeat the efforts of two years ago or would Arsenal get revenge? I obviously wanted to watch the game on television; I was looking forward to it. Then my Mum gave me some devastating news: a friend of hers was visiting from France that weekend and we would be going out for a big family lunch together, and no I could not give it a miss and stay at home to watch the football. What on earth was I going to do now? There was no way I could see the game.

I was not happy on the day of the lunch. My only solution was to take my walkman with me and try to catch bits of it on the radio. I video-recorded it at home, so I could relive another great Spurs victory later that day.

My parents must have known what was going on but our French visitors must have assumed I had terrible bladder problems. All I could think about was the match and every few minutes, even after the food had been served, I would disappear to the toilet to get the latest radio update.

After several trips to the gents, I got the dreadful news I had been fearing: Arsenal had gone a goal up, through a Tony Adams header. I stood still, almost numbed by the news. I wanted to stay and listen to the rest of the match in case Spurs got back into it, but I knew I had to return to the dinner table. I took my seat, desperately, but unsuccessfully, trying to hide my distress. One of my parents eventually asked nervously "What's the score?"

The match ended 1-0 and my disappointment was complete. It was to be the start of a long drawn out period of misery in FA Cup semi finals.

As with the semi final, I had started to listen to a lot of games on the radio. Before the days of mass television coverage and the advent of the wonderful Gillette Soccer Saturday on the addictive Sky Sports News channel, it allowed me to follow the games as they happened. I would sit in my room, listening nervously, either to the live commentary or waiting for the latest goal update from the Spurs game. The latter is almost more nerve-racking as there is that moment of uncertainty as the commentator delivers the line: "and there's been a goal at White Hart Lane". For a couple of seconds, you do not know whether you are going to be happy or sad, just certain that it will be one or the other.

Twice that season I had very uncomfortable experiences doing just this. Despite finishing eighth in the league, we had a few heavy defeats and on two occasions conceded six goals. The first of these was a 6-0 thrashing away at Sheffield United, the other a 6-2 loss at Anfield. Both of these results depressed me and, as a young teenager, caused me to sulk. I remember after the Liverpool game that my Dad noticed my troubled demeanour and asked me what was up. When I explained that we had lost 6-2 to Liverpool, he was relieved nothing serious was the matter. Of course, to me this was serious and an entirely understandable reason to be upset.

From very soon after I started following Spurs, their fortunes were able to directly affect my moods, which sometimes is really very annoying for me and those around me. To this day, the club still have the same strong power over me and the grip is showing no signs of loosening.

The following season started as usual with me trying to get my Dad to take me to some early season games. We went to Brentford again, this time for a dull and goalless pre-season friendly, and then to White Hart Lane for the match against Chelsea again. My Dad seemed to like taking me to see Chelsea, probably still harbouring secret support for them. We managed a draw this time, our goal coming from a Sheringham penalty.

Spurs were shipping managers in and out like disposable nappies and Ossie Ardiles, the old Spurs favourite and Argentinean midfielder, was installed as manager for that season. Ardiles was the type of manager Spurs fans like at their club: he had a reputation for flair and creativity, facets held in high regard at the Lane.

Soon after the Chelsea game my Tottenham supporting days were to change forever. In several of our lessons at school, the teachers wanted us to sit in alphabetical order of our surnames. I assume this was so they could remember our names more easily. I was last alphabetically in my class and was sat next to Andrew Winbourne, or Windy as he was better known. We each knew the other was a Spurs fan, but although this was the second year of being in the same class, we were not really friends.

During my least favourite lesson, Chemistry, we started talking about Spurs to cope with the boredom induced by the teacher's ramblings on molecules, the Periodic Table, or other such inconsequential details. Our teacher did not have the voice to bring the subject to life, speaking in the same dull monotone each and every lesson. After successfully whiling away most of the lesson, Windy asked "Do you want to go to a game sometime?"

I was well up for that. It meant I could go to the odd game during the season without having to ask my Dad to give up his rugby. I went home excited to give my parents the wonderful news. I was fourteen at the time and, I thought, old enough to go by myself. I also had a paper round that would enable me to buy the tickets. At that time you could get into White Hart Lane for about a fiver as a child and an all zones travelcard cost £1.50. Even if you threw in the cost of a programme, the day cost less than a tenner.

I explained all this to my parents, but, worried for my safety, they were still a little reluctant to let me go all the way to Tottenham and back. In the end, my badgering paid off and they relented, but only if I went to the lesser games (where there would be no prospect of crowd trouble) and did not wear my Spurs shirt.

So, from that conversation in my Chemistry class, I started going to see Spurs more regularly and without a parental chaperone. Our first match was against Oldham on 18th September 1993. My Dad dropped me down at Hampton Court station where I was meeting Windy. After he had pulled away in the car, I took my carefully secreted Spurs shirt from down my jeans and proudly put it on over my jumper. (I did own up to my parents later that I had done this and I wore it to every game after that.)

The journey by train from where I lived to White Hart Lane was no less time consuming than trying to get there via London's roads with my Dad. A forty minute journey to Waterloo (or Vauxhall) preceded tubes to Seven Sisters and then either a long walk up Tottenham High Road or another train to White Hart Lane station. It would have been much easier for me to support Chelsea, Fulham or Brentford, but it was a bit late for that by then.

In those days, you could just turn up on the day for games with lesser opposition and pay on the turnstiles. We did just that and sat in the East Stand lower tier. Wonderfully, within eight minutes, Spurs were 3-0 up. We were laughing, literally, after the third went in. I could not quite believe it. Never in all the previous matches I had been to had we started anywhere near as emphatically as that day. The start was due, in the main, to some appalling goalkeeping from Oldham's Paul Gerrard. He was unlucky with the first goal as the ball rebounded off the post from a Sheringham shot and hit him, sending it into the net. The next two goals were almost carbon copies of each other. Twice, Gerrard's attempted clearances, forced by the backpass law, were scuffed and fell to Spurs players. Sheringham and then Steve Sedgley each had the simple task of running the ball back unchallenged towards the goal and beating the hapless goalkeeper. Gerrard got a fair amount of stick for the rest of the game, the most common chant obviously being "dodgy 'keeper".

Jason Dozzell and Gordon Durie wrapped up an easy 5-0 victory for Spurs. Not a bad start to my new chapter of supporting Tottenham.

Windy and I went to a couple more games before the end of the calendar year. Next up was a match against Swindon Town in their one and only Premiership season. A week before the game Teddy Sheringham was badly injured at Manchester United. He was to be out of action for several months. He had been our inspiration up until that point, scoring ten goals in our opening ten league games, after being the division's top scorer the previous season. We were to miss him dearly.

At that age I had to wear glasses for things such as going to the cinema, reading off the board at school and watching live football matches. I did not wear them all the time (despite not being able to recognise people in the street until they were really quite close up) and instead carried them with me in a case. The reason was simply the vanity of a fourteen year old boy. That day, however, I wished I had just worn them. Not very cleverly, I managed to leave them on the train on the way to the Swindon game. I was more upset that I could not really see anything that was going on in the match unless it was on the touchline in front of us than I was at the fact that I had lost my glasses.

Jason Dozzell opened the scoring that day, although I had to rely on the crowd cheers to know it had gone in and Windy to tell me the scorer. Swindon equalised, and again I had to rely on the roar from the far corner of the ground to know this. It was disappointing to only score once against a team that was to concede a record breaking perfect ton of goals that season. We were also one of the few clubs to fail to register at least one win against them.

We had decided our next game would be against Leeds in November, meaning we would be going to roughly a game a month in the first part of the season. On the Friday evening before the match, while I was out delivering the free local paper (which I had started doing as a second paper round in addition to my morning deliveries to help fund going to games), I began to feel a little unwell. My first thought was the football. I decided to ignore it and hope it would go away. An early night would sort me out and ensure I woke up feeling right as rain for the match.

As it turned out, I awoke feeling dreadful, really not wanting to emerge from my bed. I was desperate to go to the game, though, and so tried to brush it aside. As Mums seem able to do, mine knew there was something wrong. Apparently, I had a fever, along with some other 'flu-like symptoms. I told her I was definitely going to the game, although I knew really that I was not up to the trip. Despite protestations, I eventually conceded that I could not go and phoned Windy to tell him the bad news. It seemed like the end of the world to me at the time. I listened, depressed, on the radio as Darren Anderton scored our goal in a 1-1 draw, wishing I was there to see it.

By the time we made it to our next game, against Norwich City two days after Christmas, we had decided to become members of the club. This allowed us to buy cheaper tickets and get tickets for the bigger games before they went on general sale. We also moved from sitting in the East Stand to the Paxton Road end behind the goal. I have been a member ever since and the Paxton Road stand was to become my regular home at the Lane for many years. After years of mostly sitting on the sides of the pitch, I wanted to get in amongst the vocal support behind the goal and feel a proper part of it all.

Our first game as members, however, did not go as planned. Norwich won 3-1, Nick Barmby scoring our solitary goal.

To make becoming members worthwhile from a monetary point of view, we had to go to enough games at the cheaper prices to break even on the initial outlay for the membership. There was only one thing for it: to go to as many games as possible before the end of the season. As a consequence, my match-attendance really got going in earnest. We went to eight out of the ten remaining home games after the Norwich match. The only ones we missed were against Coventry City on New Year's Day and against Aston Villa, which was a term-time midweek game. You could say I had become hooked.

My decision to become a regular match-goer was severely questioned and my loyalty tested through those first two months of the new year. During this time, Spurs lost a club record seven consecutive league games, of which I was at four, and went out of both cup competitions. They were two of the worst months in the club's history and they coincided with me being there regularly for the first time. Was I a jinx on the club? It was certainly something of a baptism of fire. I was still as avid a supporter as ever by the end of it though.

I would have expected a defeat to reigning League champions Manchester United anyway, so a 1-0 loss was nothing to be concerned about. By the time we came to play Sheffield Wednesday in early February, however, the defeats had been mounting up. To make matters worse we went 3-0 down. Boos were ringing out around the ground. We had played terribly and Kevin Scott, who had a particularly bad game at the centre of defence, was made the scapegoat by the fans.

Suddenly, out of the blue debutant Ronny Rosenthal got a goal back with a header from the edge of the box. We were still 3-1 down, though, and a comeback looked most unlikely. Nevertheless, the goal seemed to completely change the atmosphere inside the ground. Instead of the boos and jeers there were suddenly roars and cheers. The supporters were getting right behind the team, trying to inspire a great comeback. Looking back, this was no doubt through the shear frustration of losing all the league games of the previous month and being eliminated from both cups. The fans wanted the players to show some fight.

The noise at the back of the upper tier of the Paxton Road stand was deafening. The singing and cheering was reverberating off the roof to further accentuate the noise level. I had not heard noise like it inside a football ground before. Unfortunately, despite the best efforts of the fans, there was to be no great comeback. Although disappointed by the defeat, I left the ground on a high, awed by the noise inside White Hart Lane. I wanted to experience more of that.

The following week we suffered another expected defeat at the hands of an Alan Shearer-inspired Blackburn Rovers, who were sat in the upper echelons of the division. This sixth consecutive loss was bad enough on its own but it also meant we were being dragged towards the relegation zone. Maybe I *was* bringing bad luck to the team. Ever since the win over Oldham I had only seen bad results.

At the end of February, I went to see my second ever away game, against Chelsea. I had seen the game at White Hart Lane earlier in the season with my Dad, but this time I went with James, an old friend from school I had known for many years. We could not get tickets with the Spurs fans so we turned up on the day and sat on the benches that used to comprise the lower tier of the West Stand at Stamford Bridge. We were in among some of the hard-core Chelsea support. My Spurs shirt stayed at home.

There is a lot of rivalry surrounding this fixture and each set of fans dislikes the other intensely. Somehow I was going to have to keep my allegiance under wraps all afternoon. That was actually to prove much harder than I had thought at the outset. There were seven goals where I had to pretend to be happy when I was gutted and upset when I was overjoyed. It made for a very difficult and tiring 90 minutes.

I do not remember the exact sequence of the goals, but there were times in the game when both sides were leading. I think Spurs were 2-1 ahead through Steve Sedgley and Jason Dozzell, but any thoughts of an overdue victory were quashed as Chelsea turned it around to lead 3-2. Spurs then grabbed an equaliser as Andy Gray converted a penalty. He then contrived to miss one in the dying minutes. This was not good for my heart.

What I definitely recall is that as the game entered its final minutes the teams were level at 3-3. After the topsy-turvy nature of the match, all those defeats and having to suppress my true emotions all afternoon, I was happy to settle for this and wished for the final whistle to sound.

To my utter disbelief, however, just as the game entered the ninetieth minute, Chelsea were awarded a penalty. I was horrified. Mark Stein stepped up to confidently put the ball into the top corner. With no time for us to come back, Chelsea had won 4-3. Their fans all around me were deliriously jumping around. For the first time all

46

afternoon I could not hide my feelings. I was just standing there dumbstruck, really wishing I was not there surrounded by celebrating Chelsea supporters. Some of their fans noticed I was not joining in and looked at me in confusion, not understanding why I was not bouncing around.

I could not wait to get out of Stamford Bridge at the final whistle; I could not even really talk about the game until we were well out of Chelsea territory.

It was a new experience as a football supporter, and while in some ways I was glad I had been there, parts of me hoped never to have to go through such trauma again.

After the Chelsea game had made it seven defeats on the bounce, we did somehow manage to recover and put together a run of five games without defeat. The two I saw were draws at home to the kind of opposition we should have been looking to beat at White Hart Lane, but after the dismal start to the year any points were gratefully accepted. The first ended 2-2 against Sheffield United with goals from central defender, Kevin Scott, and Jason Dozzell. Nick Barmby got the goal in a 1-1 draw with Ipswich two weeks later.

Following his long injury lay-off, Teddy Sheringham was close to returning to fitness. He made his comeback two weeks after the Ipswich game as a substitute at Norwich at the beginning of April. We had missed him dearly all through the season and had ended up perilously close to relegation without his goals and influence. We needed him back for the final month of the season to help steer us clear of trouble. There was immense pressure on him to lift the whole team, but even I could not have imagined the impact he would actually have.

47

Two minutes after coming off the bench, and on the back of a full six months with no Premiership football, he scored Tottenham's opening goal with a shot low into the corner of the net. We went on to win the game 2-1, only our second league win of the calendar year, giving us a vital three points. Sheringham deservedly grabbed all the Easter weekend headlines following his triumphant return.

Indeed, he scored again just two days later in the Easter Monday game with West Ham, this time with a penalty. What he could not do was prevent the Hammers scoring four of their own in an embarrassing home display.

Spurs lost twice more before I saw them again at home to Southampton. With four games to go, we were still in danger of being relegated, something that had previously been unthinkable for me. We needed some points desperately; another run of defeats like earlier in the campaign would most likely see us go down.

It was with great relief, therefore, that we managed to record a 3-0 victory. In a traumatic season, it was the first win I had seen since the trouncing of Oldham back in September, and it was our second biggest win of the season. Sedgley, Samways and Anderton got the goals that meant we had a little bit of breathing space as we entered the final week of the season. One win out of the three remaining games would ensure we stayed in the top flight. Of course, this was easier said than done.

The first opportunity was wasted away at Wimbledon. The game was only memorable for me as it was the first time I had sat with the Spurs fans at an away game, something I later came to love. But this time all I was able to concentrate on was the result. Another

Sheringham penalty was rendered useless as we proceeded to concede twice. There were just two games left to save ourselves.

When you really need a result to get out of relegation trouble, the last thing you want is to play another team fighting for their lives, in front of their passionate crowd, on a wet and muddy pitch on a midweek evening. That was what we were faced with, however. Do not get me wrong; I would not have wanted to play Manchester United, but a mid-table team with nothing to play for would have been nice.

We had to play Oldham away on the last Thursday of the season. It was never going to be as easy as our 5-0 win over them back in September (a game that seemed a long time ago by then) and so it proved.

I was proud to be a Tottenham supporter that night. All too often Spurs lost to battling, scrappy teams and this occasion was a prime example of a match they might not fancy. Listening on the radio, though, the team proved me wrong. We battled and scrapped ourselves to a 2-0 win, and to safety, on an utter quagmire of a pitch. I was jumping around my bedroom with delight when the goals went in.

Relegation would have been awful, even more so in the modern game now with all the financial consequences. It is a great fear of mine. Every now and then Spurs make life interesting for their fans by getting dangerously close to the drop, sometimes even occupying one of the bottom three places for a while, as if to get you really worried. They have always managed to get out to safety by the end of the season though.

It would be disastrous to go down. I would still go to my usual quota of games of course, in the hope of seeing a quick return to the top flight, but there would not be the same week-in week-out excitement during the time you were in the lower leagues. Playing Crewe and Rotherham, while not meaning to sound at all disrespectful, would not get the heart racing or the atmosphere going in the same way games against Arsenal and Manchester United would. Obviously not all Premiership games are classics and you get your fair share of excitement-filled matches in the lower divisions, but the glamour and the top prizes are not there. Luckily, I have not had to cope with such an outcome in my supporting life, and I sincerely hope I never have to. Unfortunately, there is probably much more chance of that happening than us becoming Champions.

The final home game of the season was somewhat of an anti-climax. Part of me had wanted the team to slip up at Oldham so that I would be able to see and be part of our efforts to stay up on a tension-filled last day. That was a risky wish, and most of me was quite content that we had climbed to safety already. Having ensured we would be playing in the Premiership the following season, the exertions of the Oldham game looked to have taken their toll against QPR just two days later. We lost 2-1, Sheringham scoring our only goal, but it made little difference. The day was all about being able to relax at the Lane for the first time in months. A win would have been nice but the season's goal, as it progressed, had been achieved. The players did their lap of honour, and in the end deserved their applause.

The turning point of the season had been Sheringham's injury. From the moment it happened we began to slide down the table. The statistics suggest we could have experienced an entirely different campaign had he been in the team throughout. He played in 19 league games, scoring 14 goals. We won 11 league games all season; Sheringham played in eight of them. The fact that we only won three times during his long absence shows how much we relied on him.

In my first season going to see Tottenham regularly, I had seen just two wins in fifteen games, hardly a ratio to entice me back. We finished 15th in the league table, the joint worst league placing (with the 1991/92 season) in all my time supporting the club. The thing was I loved it; I had got a proper taste for it after Christmas despite all the defeats. The ups and downs and the emotional torment and joy meant I wanted to be back as much as possible once the new season started.

3. Walking in a Klinsmann wonderland ...

Some people remember where they were when Kennedy was shot, or when they heard Princess Diana had died, or even when England won the World Cup. I remember where I was when I heard Jurgen Klinsmann had joined Tottenham Hotspur Football Club. In July 1994, I was on one of my many annual two-week family holidays in France. As always during the busy summers of transfer activity, it was important to keep up to date with the comings and goings while I was out of the country. We were staying in a remote house that year and, as usual, the only way of finding out the sports news was the BBC World Service on the radio. I was listening to this one afternoon in the kitchen of our rented accommodation, waiting for the football headlines, the first of which was the incredible news that Tottenham Hotspur had signed Jurgen Klinsmann. I could not believe it. I must have misheard or maybe the newsreader had got the team wrong. It was true though: a truly world class player had signed for Spurs. Klinsmann at White Hart Lane. I was over the moon. Hearing this news was probably my most exciting moment as a football fan outside of a match. After getting a taste for being a fairly regular part of the White Hart Lane crowd the previous season and with my membership all sorted for the coming season, I was looking forward to August and Klinsmann's first home game with immense excitement.

The 1994/95 campaign still remains my most enjoyable season watching Spurs. It was my first full season as a member, and the prospect of seeing the team regularly throughout a season for the first time, coupled with Klinsmann's arrival, meant that I could not wait for the first home game of the season. As well as myself and Windy, two other school friends, James (who I had been to Chelsea with a few months previously) and Stuart, had become members during the summer and the four of us regularly went to the games together. I still go to my games now with James and Stu.

Unfortunately, there was a sour note to the start of the campaign. Spurs were to go into the season with six points deducted (originally twelve but reduced on appeal) and banned from playing in the FA Cup for that year, as punishment for financial irregulations. Alan Sugar had vowed to fight this, and it was widely expected that the FA would overturn their original overly-harsh decisions. Nevertheless, all this was hanging over the first few months of the season like a bad stench. If the punishments remained in place, the season was almost pointless, with survival in the Premier League the only realistic objective.

Ossie Ardiles, a supremely skilful playmaker at Spurs in the seventies and eighties, started his second season as manager determined to play attractive attacking football, something that would eventually turn out to be his downfall. He structured his team to be spearheaded by a five-pronged attacking force of Darren Anderton, Nick Barmby, Ilie Dumitrescu, Teddy and Jurgen. Obviously, once the goalkeeper and defence were taken into account, this meant there were few, if any, players in the midfield.

The opening game of the season, away to Sheffield Wednesday, was an exciting 4-3 win for Spurs, with Klinsmann getting his first goal for the club. Jurgen the German, as he was sometimes referred to, was as renowned for diving almost as much as he was for his football talent. Upon arriving at White Hart Lane, he was obviously aware of this and attempted to laugh off this part of his reputation from the outset. He announced in a pre-season press conference that he had joined a local diving school, but it was his pre-planned celebrations for his first Spurs goal that really endeared him to people. When he scored against Sheffield Wednesday he ran to the side of the pitch and took a full-length dive, arms outstretched, across the turf, closely followed by all his team-mates doing exactly the same thing. Even the goalkeeper, Ian Walker, ran the full length of the pitch to get involved. This was captured by all the photographers there that day, and the image of Jurgen's dive was splashed across the papers on the Sunday morning. Jurgen had arrived.

This 4-3 win whet my appetite even further for the first home game, which, luckily, was only four days later against Everton. This being a school night in my GCSE year, getting the train from Hampton, on the edge of south west London, to Tottenham in north London was not a favourable option. So that we could go to the match, my Dad offered to get himself a ticket in the West Stand and drive us there and back. He did this a few times over a couple of years, something I am very grateful for, and of course he got to see the super Spurs play, which I am sure he was grateful for!

My friends and I were sat in the Paxton Road upper tier, behind the goal, and the atmosphere was one of anticipation. Spurs were having the better of the first half when Klinsmann produced another one of his party pieces. The ball was jumping around in the Everton penalty area, eventually falling kindly for Jurgen, who unleashed a powerful acrobatic overhead volley into the corner of the goal. White Hart Lane erupted and cue the team dive again by way of celebration. Klinsmann scored again, this time with a header and the match ended 2-1 to Spurs. A maximum six points to start the season and things were looking promising.

I then saw Spurs lose a couple of times after that, first narrowly 1-0 to Manchester United and then convincingly 4-1 to Nottingham Forest. Ardiles's tactics were not working. Our attacking potential was not being fulfilled and the defence and midfield were unable to cope with the emphasis on attack. Teddy Sheringham also managed the feat of missing a penalty in three consecutive home games, starting with one against Everton. Even though we managed to get a 2-1 win at Wimbledon and a draw at home to QPR, Ossie Ardiles's reign was brought to an abrupt end by a worried Board. His last game in charge was the 3-1 home win against West Ham. Three brilliantly worked goals from Klinsmann, Sheringham and Barmby and a hard-working performance left me wondering whether Ossie had finally got it right, and that sacking him was a little premature.

His replacement was Gerry Francis, who left the manager's job at QPR to join us. It was hoped he would bring slightly more controlled tactics to the team, building a solid defence, while still allowing our strikers to do the business. His first game in charge showed that he had a long way to go to achieve this. Spurs went 3-0 down after just half an hour at home to Aston Villa. Somehow the team battled back to 3-3 with goals from the same three players that scored against West Ham; we also had chances to win it. Still, a draw was a fair (and somewhat unexpected at one stage) result. As we often did in the closing moments of a match to ensure a quick escape to White Hart Lane train station, we made our way out to the gangway behind the seats in the Paxton Road lower tier to watch the last couple of minutes of injury time run their course. Just as we did this, Villa's Dean Saunders broke into the penalty area and fired the winner into the corner of the net. I could not believe this after the players had worked so hard to get back level. I kicked the wall in frustration.

After that first home game against Everton, where we sat in the upper tier of the Paxton Road end, we spent most of the rest of the season in the lower tier of the same stand. Paxton Road was at the north end of the ground and the stand was designated the members stand, which meant we could get preferential tickets at a reduced price. As 15 year-olds, and therefore junior members, the price of tickets was a little over a fiver. Residing behind the goal meant we were in among the singing fans and, therefore, the White Hart Lane atmosphere. Sitting in the lower tier meant that we were also close to the action: we would buy seats as close to the front row as possible.

After recording our first clean sheet of the season in a 0-0 draw with Chelsea at the end of November, we played Newcastle at home at the beginning of December. A 4-2 win turned out to be the best performance of the season so far. Teddy Sheringham scored a hatrick and was superb throughout. It was probably rather unfair that he was overshadowed by the brilliance of Klinsmann that season. Teddy was the ideal foil for Jurgen and they worked almost perfectly in tandem, hitting it off almost immediately. Jurgen later said that Teddy Sheringham was the best striker he had played with in his long and glittering career. Some praise indeed.

As we were walking from White Hart Lane train station to the ground before the game, we were stopped and asked for a short interview with Cock-a-Doodle-Doo, a Spurs fanzine. I think the topic was what we thought of the recent arrival of Gerry Francis as manager. We also had our photo taken, which was to be in the next edition of the fanzine, along with our insightful comments. The photo published shows four slightly awkward-looking, slightly drunk teenagers in matching blue and white Santa hats with the slogan "Santa Scores for Spurs". It was only three weeks until Christmas after all.

The reason we were slightly drunk was due to our recently devised pre-match ritual. As you do when you are about 15 or 16, we had started to experiment with alcohol. We did not like the taste of beer, though, so we would drink a sweeter alternative, cider, instead. The oldest looking of us, Windy, would stop at his local off-licence on the way to Hampton Court train station, our meeting place. We would get there well in advance of the train we needed to catch, and sit behind the station buildings rapidly drinking our bottles of Diamond White or 'K' extra strong cider. All very classy. We would then start our train journey to White Hart Lane slightly out-of-it. The alcohol had largely, but not completely, worn off by the time the match had started.

A week after the Newcastle game, we played Sheffield Wednesday at home. The Friday before the game, the FA had overturned their original punishments, and Spurs had their six points and place in the

FA Cup back. There was a celebratory atmosphere at the Lane and Alan Sugar received a standing ovation before kick off for his efforts in getting the punishments revoked. A couple of years previously this would have been unthinkable following his public battle for the club with Spurs favourite Terry Venables.

The atmosphere was great and a 3-1 win fuelled the party. All the Spurs songs about going to Wembley were sung now that we had the chance to get there. Chris Waddle was also returning to Spurs, playing for Wednesday that day. I wished he had never left Spurs and I did not really understand why at the time, but Spurs needed the money and he had the chance to play for a top European club. When he took a corner in front of us at the Spurs end, I shouted towards him (probably encouraged by the cider), politely enquiring why he had left.

Sheffield Wednesday were out to spoil the party though and led 1-0 at half time, deservedly so. I was still convinced, however, that my pre-match prediction of a 3-1 win would come to fruition. It did thanks to three goals in the last half hour. Undoubtedly the best of the three was a superb powerful half-volley into the top corner from 20 yards out by Klinsmann. The Lane went crazy at this goal, myself especially included. It was a great day, a great atmosphere and a great win.

On the evening of 2nd January 1995, I experienced my first north London derby, a match I will always remember. It was less than a week after a drab post-Christmas 0-0 draw with Crystal Palace and the games could not have been more different. It was a bitterly cold evening but the ground was warmed by the pre-match atmosphere and illuminated by the floodlights. The singing started 45 minutes before kick off and continued solidly throughout the match. On our way to the ground from the train station, the Sky TV cameras filmed us as part of a larger group singing "we love you Tottenham". You could just see me on the television at the back of the group. "Glory, Glory Tottenham Hotspur" was sung before the game and continued right up until kick off. All the Spurs supporters were so fired up. This was all new to me and I was enjoying every second of it, trying to take it all in. I had guessed that the supporters' behaviour and the atmosphere were probably like this at all north London derbies, not just that evening. In later years, I was proved right and became aware of an entirely different atmosphere, a far more intense atmosphere, that accompanies games against Arsenal compared with that at other games.

The match itself was not that entertaining; both teams worked and battled very hard, another common trait of north London derbies. Not much was coming off for Klinsmann despite his workmanlike efforts. The fans contested every decision, whether it was correct or not, and all Arsenal songs were drowned out by a Spurs version, something that rarely happens at other Spurs home games. Whenever Arsenal were on top, the Spurs fans would be up and shouting, encouraging the players.

There was only one goal in the game and our Romanian midfielder, Gica Popescu, scored it, slotting in from 12 yards following a swift attack and cross from the right. The goal was celebrated like no other I had witnessed before, everybody jumping around aimlessly and shouting with euphoria until we were out of breath. The song of the evening soon became "one-nil to the Tottenham", copying Arsenal's well-used version, to the tune of Go West by the Pet Shop Boys. Late in the game, Klinsmann almost added a second. In fact, we all thought he had from where we were sat, prompting that slightly embarrassing brief roar and then silence that accompanies such situations.

Despite the game itself not being a classic, this was the best football occasion I had ever been part of. The atmosphere was amazing throughout and the crowd were so animated to watch. The celebratory singing continued onto the street and in the queue for the train. Actually, I wished we had stayed in the stadium for longer after the game to enjoy the party, but we had a train to catch. The win over Arsenal meant that Spurs were now unbeaten in nine games and had kept five consecutive clean sheets.

A week later, I went to my first FA Cup match. An FA Cup campaign that season was a welcome and unexpected bonus, and I looked forward to seeing Spurs in the competition they are most famously associated with. However, this match was a disappointing introduction to the Cup for me. We were playing non-league Altrincham, and everyone knew Spurs would win, which resulted in a dull atmosphere around the ground. Such was the expectation, some supporters did not even stand up when the second or third goals went in. There was no real competition between either the players or the fans. The game was almost a side issue for the supporters, who were still celebrating the Arsenal win and singing about the cup run to follow this tie. Spurs won comfortably 3-0, but as so often happens when top teams play non-league sides, Spurs tried to over-play and over-pass and so did not show the superiority they should have. I realise this may sound arrogant, but in games like this you almost want the non-league team to score, just so that the team (especially their scorer) and their supporters have something to celebrate in a famous stadium and treasure for the rest of their career as a player or fan. Altrincham did actually have the ball in the net, but it was disallowed, the linesman signalling a foul throw that the referee did not see until all the Altrincham players were celebrating. At full time shirts were exchanged so that the Altrincham players would have a memento of the day; some of their players were indicating that they also wanted to swap shorts. That would probably be going too far and thankfully did not happen. My experience of the FA Cup first hand had started; I would have quite a few memories of, and feelings towards, it over the coming years.

A week after the Altrincham game, we saw a 2-1 win away at West Ham. It was similar to the Sheffield Wednesday game in that we went behind in the first half, but came back well in the second to secure the win with goals from Sheringham and Klinsmann. The atmosphere and rivalry between the fans was intense, almost generating as good an atmosphere as at the Arsenal game.

Spurs were playing well, scoring goals and winning games. It was a great time to be watching them, and be a part of White Hart Lane. By this time, we had enticed a few more school friends to get memberships and come to games; sometimes there were as many as seven of us sat in a row. A week after beating the League leaders Blackburn Rovers 3-1 at home, we went into a game away at the old nemesis Chelsea highly confident. Even on top form and with Chelsea not the dominant force they are now, we could not carve out a win. The bogey team remained so. Spurs probably did deserve to win this match: Darren Anderton hit a post and we had a host of other chances. Sheringham scored our only goal, though, in a 1-1 draw.

As a Tottenham Hotspur supporter I love going to White Hart Lane and relish the feeling of walking out into the stadium. I feel at home there. However, going to away games gives you an entirely different experience. As an away supporter, you are in the minority and only the really passionate and loyal supporters tend to follow the team away. In the away end there is a real camaraderie, a mutual respect that you are a "real" Spurs fan who follows the team around the country. Away fans nearly always vocally support the team, providing backing and encouragement in most circumstances, however bad. This contrasts with the home support, where Spurs fans have a reputation, sometimes justified in the past, of being a little fickle and getting on the players' backs. (This does not actually seem to be the case nowadays and the home support, along with that away, is among the best in the country.) Being the minority at another team's ground and among the die-hard fans results in a passionate, loud, supportive atmosphere. It is fantastic to be a part of. The level of the atmosphere is heightened further at away games in London. As a supporter, if pushed, I would say I prefer the occasion of an away match more than a match at White Hart Lane.

Unfortunately, we could not get tickets in the Spurs end for the Chelsea game. Instead we braved the temporary seating that was installed at the Shed end of Stamford Bridge at the time. The usual wearing of my Spurs shirt was abandoned and I even secreted a Chelsea scarf upon my person, just in case I needed to prove I was a Chelsea fan. Scary bunch, that lot in the Shed. We had all heard the stories of violent fans giving opposition supporters a 'Chelsea smile'. I was quite happy with my own grin thank you very much.

I did not enjoy sitting with the Chelsea fans that day: being among the home fans takes away all the good things about an away match that I have just described. Nowadays, I would not pay to sit with the home supporters at an away game for that reason. The problem was that you had to pretend to be a Chelsea fan, something I probably could not do convincingly. When Spurs scored the opening goal, to let out the joy inside, I found myself shouting against Spurs, just as many Chelsea fans around us were. However, when Chelsea scored their equaliser, I could not quite bring myself to cheer and jump around, instead standing still, looking around, and seeing several others doing the same. I reckon there were quite a lot of Spurs fans in the Shed that day. Our approach to not revealing our Spurs allegiances that day was justified. When Spurs scored the first goal, the Spurs section started singing "one-nil to the Tottenham"; I heard one friendly Chelsea fan behind us say "it'll be one-nil to us in the streets afterwards."

Around this time, we had started hanging around the players' entrance after games in the hope of meeting the players and getting some autographs. At an age when there was not much we could do on a Saturday evening anyway, we would often hang around until all the players and managers had left the stadium. This sometimes kept us there until about 7pm. It was an aim of the season to get all the Spurs players to sign my Spurs shirt. Most players were happy to oblige, and even have a short chat. Some players, however, including Klinsmann, were completely elusive, something we thought was a little rude at the time given all the support they were receiving from us. After the Chelsea game, I shook Teddy Sheringham's hand and said "good goal Ted", to which he replied simply "thanks". These are the sorts of nice touches that superstar players can give to slightly obsessive teenage fans.

At the time of writing this book, some ten years after that brief interaction, I saw Teddy in a pub in Richmond-upon-Thames one Friday evening. As he was a bit of a hero of mine, and spurred on by several beverages, I decided to go over and speak to him. I blurted out something along the lines of "Teddy, I just wanted to say I have the utmost respect for your career. I hope West Ham (his current club) do well this season and I was a big fan when you were at Spurs". His expression did not change as he mumbled "thanks" and then he turned away again. I walked away, knowing deep down I had just made a complete fool of myself. He probably just wanted a quiet night at the pub (with the attractive young woman he was with) and not to be disturbed by slightly tipsy fans, but for me such attention is something that players should not only be prepared to accept but also respond to graciously. Football as a professional sport is nothing without fans and so it follows that professional football players would not enjoy the status they have today without the fans. I resisted spurting out "I paid your wages once" and scuttled back off to the group of friends I was out with. Disgruntled that the Teddy Sheringham did not want to speak to me, the Olly Wright, I texted a few football friends. James helpfully replied with the advice to "rugby tackle him buddy. That ought to get his attention". With all the attention he was getting he left early. I did not see him join the crowd on the dancefloor and dance wildly to Bryan Adams or Mustang Sally.

Colin Calderwood, although never spectacular, was a solid central defender and a cult figure among our group of four. When we saw him outside Stamford Bridge, we told him to look out for us at the next game, telling him where we would be sitting, including the exact seat numbers. He smiled. Surely he would remember these crazy boys a week later!

Colin definitely did not remember us. Understandably he showed no interest in the four boys shouting at him from the stands, instead preferring to get on with the game. I have always wondered what the players can hear from the stands (and what they choose not to hear). Managers and players always talk about the "twelfth man", referring to the overall support and atmosphere generated by the fans. But do they actually know when you are singing their name? They must do; I would deliberately listen out for the sound of 30,000 people singing my name, just to try to make out whether it was nice or not. Surely it must spur a player on to do well with that force of backing.

Anyway, the game where Calderwood ruthlessly ignored us was the fifth round of the FA Cup at home to Southampton; three weeks earlier we had knocked out Sunderland, beating them 4-1 away from home. There was the usual cup atmosphere, with the variety of Wembley songs being sung in good voice. The match was fairly uneventful, ending 1-1, which was a fair result. The replay, however, was to be spectacular. We did not go to the game as it was a midweek away game on a school night, but I was able to watch the match at home on Sky Sports. Gerry Francis decided to man-mark Southampton maestro Matt Le Tissier, and the players obviously neglected the other Southampton players as they went 2-0 up. At half time the manager changed the tactics and we managed to get back to 2-2 by the end of the 90 minutes and take the game into extra time, where we scored four times. The remarkable 6-2 victory is most remembered, rightly so, for Ronny Rosenthal's outrageous hatrick, each goal scored from ridiculous angles or distances. He always ran about like a headless chicken on amphetamines, and was responsible for one of the misses of the decade when playing for Liverpool, but he was a Spurs cult hero after that game.

In between the two games, we contrived to lose 2-1 at home to Wimbledon. It was not the best of games, but we deserved the win nonetheless. We had so many shots at goal, fifteen corners to Wimbeldon's two and three good penalty appeals turned down. The Daily Telegraph described the referee as being "on a different planet". The most amusing aspect of the day was revelling in George Graham's sacking from Arsenal allegedly for accepting illegal payments in transfer deals. "Old George, he likes a bung" was the verse from the terraces. I am sure not a single Spurs fans would have believed then that he would one day be the manager of Tottenham Hotspur Football Club.

A few days after the Southampton replay, I went to my first away match outside London. Myself and Windy travelled on the Spurs coaches up to Nottingham Forest for a league fixture. I used these official Spurs coaches for travelling to all the away games I went to while I was still at school. They were good value for money and convenient in that they took you straight to the away ground. They provided ideal hassle-free travel for youngsters like me or, especially, those fans who lived near Tottenham. For me, the coach trips meant a full day out. It took about an hour and a half to get the variety of trains and tubes needed to reach White Hart Lane. Also, with the coach trip by nature a slow journey, it meant I spent from the early morning until the late evening travelling to spend two hours inside a football stadium. If I look at it rationally, this was a crazy waste of time, but I loved these away games and being part of the travelling support, and so did not resent the travel at all.

I remember it felt exciting getting a police escort to and from the ground; it made you feel part of an important group of people. Forest fans and locals looked at the trail of coaches, making me really feel part of the Tottenham support. The coaches allowed an excessive, some may say safe, amount of time to reach away grounds, which usually meant you were in the stadium at least an hour before kick off. This resulted in lots of Spurs fans being in the ground early, though, so the pre-match atmosphere would build quite a time before kick off. Against Forest, as all the players came out to warm up, the appropriate song for each player was sung. There were also many Wembley songs as our FA Cup campaign was gathering momentum.

I felt I was now finally getting to know most of the Spurs songs, which was important for me in feeling a proper part of the Spurs crowd. The lack of really regular visits to Spurs games before the previous season, and in those visits sitting away from the main vocal support, meant that over the last few months I had been gradually learning all the Spurs verses. There are a lot to learn too: there are songs unique to Spurs as a club, a variety of songs fitted to the top players' names, songs common to all clubs with the words adjusted for Spurs, and new and spontaneous songs created for events that had happened in the recent past. I particularly remember taunting the Forest fans, who were in the tier above us, with "there's only one Des Walker", commemorating his winning own-goal in the extra time of the 1991 FA Cup Final.

Ronny received the biggest cheer of the day after his FA Cup heroics. We had a new chant for him and whenever he got a touch of the ball we obviously shouted "shoot!" no matter where he was on the pitch.

The game itself was very average until the last 13 minutes, when Sheringham scored for Tottenham, right in front of us. I was so happy, thinking I was going to witness a win in my first away game outside London. Within a few minutes, however, Forest were winning 2-1. I could not believe it. I sat back in my seat, with my head in my hands. Why were Spurs doing this to me? But some fans started singing, despite the likely defeat, and everyone, including myself, joined in. This would rarely, if ever, have happened at a home game of similar stature. I thought it was fantastic, though, the fans fighting to the end. I like to think the players were lifted by this never-say-die attitude of the supporters, and with a couple of minutes to go, Colin Calderwood popped up to prod home an equaliser. The Spurs stand went mad, jubilant that we had snatched a draw, even though we thought we had secured a win 10 minutes previously. The Spurs supporters felt that they had been directly responsible for the equalising goal and were celebrating accordingly. The singing continued past the full time whistle, and I remember thinking how much I loved being part of these away games; I wanted to go to more.

Among all the exciting, exhilarating matches, there are equally as many, both wins and losses, that fail to reel you in in the same way. These games are usually at home, where the opposition are considered poor and where the resulting atmosphere is dulled and subdued. Goals are not celebrated with the usual enthusiasm because they are expected. There is a lack of tension. When you watch Spurs several times a season, and so do not have the awe factor of when seeing them infrequently, these matches become, to be honest, fairly boring. The games often pass by without incident, but you still want to go, to be part of it, and, I suppose, so you fully appreciate the exhilarating matches that get your heart racing. One thing you hope for against lesser opposition, though, is goals.

One such match was at home to Ipswich Town, four days after the Nottingham trip. Spurs won easily 3-0 without playing well. Ipswich had lost 9-0 to Manchester United in their previous match, and so to their supporters only losing 3-0 was almost a victory. We applauded their witty song "3-0, we only lost 3-0". You have to laugh in the face of adversity sometimes as a football supporter.

A couple of weeks later, I left another one of these 'easy' home games (against Leicester City) about 20 minutes early. The game was 0-0 and we went to queue for tickets for a forthcoming away game, thinking others would be doing the same. In those days tickets for most of the away games went on sale straight after the final whistle of a preceding home game, which made getting out of the ground promptly extremely important some weeks. On this occasion, I think we were concerned at the small allocation we had received. Annoyingly, we were actually stood by ourselves for about 15 minutes with no-one else around. In this time Spurs scored the winning goal, at least I assumed it was a Spurs goal from the noise. It was slightly eerie stood outside the ground as the noise from the stadium filtered out. I simply held my arms aloft, a more subdued reaction than had I still been in my seat, surrounded by other Spurs fans. We were told afterwards that Jurgen had scored with another of his spectacular overhead kicks.

By the time of this game, some of our pre-match cider drinking had got out of hand. James had been violently sick in McDonalds before the Southampton cup game and had to miss the first part of the match to sober up. Before the Leicester game, however, Windy took things to the extreme. He had drunk countless cans of 'K' extra strong cider by the time we had to carry him up Tottenham High Road from Seven Sisters tube station. When we stopped half way up the High Road to get our usual McDonalds lunch, we tried to prop him up by the entrance while we ordered our food. He promptly fell flat on his face, to the amusement of our fellow diners. He had hardly improved by the time we reached the ground, was refused entry by a steward and was quickly arrested for drunk and disorderly behaviour. Windy spent the match in a cell in Tottenham Police Station and was cautioned. Our cider sessions waned a lot after that, although we still had a couple of cans before a game to warm our spirits.

Sandwiched between the Ipswich and Leicester games was the other Spurs match I did not go to but wished I could have more than any other, apart from that FA Cup semi final against Arsenal in 1991. I did not even think about going to that game; it was not an option in my mind as a twelve year-old boy. This match, however, an FA Cup quarter final tie away at Anfield, I was planning on getting a ticket for. I was looking forward to a big away trip after the recent match at Nottingham Forest and this was a massive game. What I did not realise was that they would all be snapped up by the season ticket holders, who had priority over members. I was bitterly disappointed.

The only option was to listen to the game on the radio, as I did with all the games I did not attend. Capital Gold 1548AM was my station of choice, as it focussed on the London clubs and I loved the extravagant and passionate commentating of Jonathan Pearce, their main man.

Tottenham have an unenviable awful record at Anfield and Liverpool were the big favourites. Nevertheless, there was always hope, a necessary weapon for the football supporter as I have said before, and several thousand Spurs fans had made the trip to Liverpool to take their places behind the goal in the Anfield Road stand. I was extremely jealous of all of them.

Listening to football matches on the radio is an excruciatingly nerve-racking experience. You have to rely on the commentator to tell you everything that is going on, and from this you attempt to visualise the game. You are never entirely sure where the players or ball are or how dangerous a particular situation is. Whenever there is a goalmouth melee, you are never quite sure what is happening, who has the ball or where it is. At least with televised or live matches you know exactly when to be nervous. Still, I spent many hours in my bedroom listening to midweek Spurs games and away games at the weekend.

I listened to this FA Cup tie, as usual, in my bedroom, never keeping still, sometimes lying on my bed, sometimes pacing round the room, and often kicking a sponge tennis ball around, pretending to score a vital goal against my bed.

As expected, Liverpool took the lead through Robbie Fowler. The hope intensified but deep down I feared the worst. Then, just before half time Klinsmann laid the ball off to Sheringham on the edge of the box, who curled a delicious shot in off the top of the post from 20 yards. I jumped around my room in silent jubilation, as I nearly always did, for fear of embarrassment with my family elsewhere in the house,

71

which was silly really. I would quite happily show my true emotions to hundreds of Spurs fans around me each week, so why not at home? I guess the difference is simply that in the ground everyone is doing the same as you.

With two minutes to go, the score remained 1-1. I was happy with this; a draw at Anfield was a good result and now there would be a quarter final replay at White Hart Lane that I could go to and witness, hopefully, Spurs progressing to the semi final. With these thoughts floating around my head, Sheringham flicked the ball through to Jurgen bearing down on goal. Jonathon Pearce does not commentate on goals half-heartedly, preferring to yell and shout and rely on his spontaneity to carry him through the moment. Klinsmann was through and I braced myself in front of the radio. I can still hear the words "… Klinsmann has done it, Jurgen Klinsmann has won the tie for Tottenham Hotspur, two minutes to go …"

I was jumping round my room again, this time shouting with delight. I came to a stop, lying on the floor with my arms aloft. We were in the semi final, a game I had to get to after this. I was ecstatic, but at the same time wished I could have been part of that bouncing euphoric mass of Spurs fans I later saw on Match of the Day. Various accounts of this match written by Spurs fans who were there that day describe it as one of their favourite moments supporting the club, and I agree. I have been getting shivers up my spine writing my account of it now.

A week and a half after this momentous cup tie, Spurs and Liverpool played out a goalless draw at White Hart Lane. While the Liverpool fans applauded Klinsmann for his efforts ten days previously, the Spurs fans taunted them with "where were you when

Klinsmann scored?" I think if I were to choose the team I supported based purely on the friendliness of the fans, based on the supporters I have encountered, I would support Liverpool. Disappointingly, instead of revelling in the recent cup win, Spurs fans focussed much of their attention on Neil Ruddock, a central defender who had left Spurs for Liverpool a couple of years previously, greeting him with chants of "Judas" and booing him whenever he touched the ball. The negative dominated when the atmosphere should have been a positive one. All I wanted to do was to continue celebrating the quarter final win. When Ruddock gave away a penalty, which Klinsmann missed anyway, the chants reverted to "there's only one Neil Ruddock".

A week before the FA Cup semi final, I made the short trip down to the Dell at Southampton for an 11.30 kick off. The Dell is one of the worst top-flight grounds I have been to, with awful facilities and one small stand that sloped from left to right so it fitted in the residential area. It did, however, have much more character and a better atmosphere than their current modern stadium at St. Mary's. Spurs lost a seven-goal thriller 4-3 in a match that was full of excitement if not quality. The obvious excuse for the loss and the performance was that their minds were on the upcoming semi final. If the players' minds were elsewhere, I think the same could have been said of the fans. There was not the usual away match atmosphere, although there were many Wembley songs. I was excited about the forthcoming semi final, although at that stage I still did not know if I would be going. Tickets for members were going on sale in the coming week on a first-come, first-serve basis.

Luckily it was the school Easter holidays so I had the opportunity of going up to Tottenham early on the day they went on sale. James and I had decided to arrive about three hours before the tickets were to go on sale to ensure we were nicely near the front of the queue. We walked up to the Paxton Road end of the ground, from where the tickets were being sold, and as we turned the corner we were greeted with a huge line of Spurs fans stretching back as far as we could see. We had somewhat foolishly been sure we would be some of the first people there and so guaranteed tickets. There were thousands of fans there already. We walked down the queue in disbelief, wondering where the end would be. Was it right round the stadium? Would we now get tickets? We joined the end of the queue about half way down the East Stand, and waited nervously for the ticket office to open. Please let there be enough tickets, I was thinking. Finally the ticket office opened and cries of "Spurs are on their way to Wembley" rang out from the patiently waiting fans. The queue moved quite quickly and we actually got tickets comfortably, as did many people behind us. We were going to the FA Cup semi final. It would be by far the biggest Spurs match I had been to and I felt so happy to be going.

Thanks to whoever makes these sorts of decisions, whether it be the police, FA, television or the clubs, the game was a 1.00pm kick off in Leeds, which meant a ridiculously early departure from White Hart Lane on the coaches. There were no trains early enough to get us to north London on time, so my Dad kindly drove us round the North Circular. It was a quick drive at about 5.30am.

Scores of coaches left White Hart Lane that morning, full of supporters as dismissive of the early hour as me, and all adorned with flags, scarves and posters. The Spurs contingent were on their way and we would be noticed. The volume of traffic around Leeds was huge, and as a result we only got into Elland Road about 30 minutes before kick off. The party atmosphere was already underway as we made our way to our seats, the fans equipped with scarves, flags, balloons and their best singing voices. We should have arrived about an hour earlier, and been able to fully soak up the pre-match build-up. The first thing that struck me was that Everton had three sides of the ground; the Spurs supporters filled the massive stand on one side of the pitch. This meant that Everton would be always attacking their own fans and the noise from them was coming from three directions, compared with just one from the Spurs fans. The Daily Telegraph report the next day described the resulting atmosphere as having a "Goodison air".

The party and the singing continued right up until kick off. As the players entered the pitch they were greeted by showers of confetti and balloons. As we often did at the Lane, we had ripped up the several newspapers that had helped pass some of the journey earlier that day, and the remains were ready for when the teams emerged. The stadium was awash with blue and white, those being the colours of both teams. This was it. The FA Cup semi final. We were there.

Spurs were big favourites after the Liverpool win, with Everton placed towards the bottom of the league, while Spurs were sitting safely in the top half. A dream final of Spurs v Manchester United was widely predicted. On top of all this, Everton are one of those teams that Spurs always without fail do well against. The Merseysiders did not really stand a chance. A Klinsmann-led Tottenham would emulate the Gascoigne-inspired Tottenham of 1991 and reach the FA Cup final.

Among all this expectation, there was a buzz of excitement floating round the stadium as the kick off was greeted by a roar from both sets of fans. The atmosphere was superb and I had never heard such vociferous and positive support from a set of Spurs fans. Everyone was joining in and I was shouting out the songs at the top of my voice.

Unfortunately, Everton had not read the script. Inspired by their three-pronged support, they went into a 2-0 lead. Spurs were playing dreadfully, and Ian Walker, our goalkeeper, gifted them their second goal. This was a disaster. The eternal hope of a football supporter remained, though. The response to being 2-0 down was to stand up and try to encourage the players with our support. In the face of adversity, the Spurs fans were staying strong. There was one particularly loud, prolonged and forceful rendition of "come on you Spurs", with each and every fan's fists thrusting towards the pitch, as if to give the players the extra energy they so desperately needed. Spurs were pinned into their own half for much of the game, but whenever there was any promising attack, it was accompanied with supporters standing up and shouting encouragement.

Even at 2-0 I felt we could still get back into it, either by a flash of genius or a piece of luck. We had come from behind in previous rounds after all. Then, we were awarded a debatable penalty. The piece of luck had arrived; the comeback would start here. The relief was there for all to see among the fans and the players. Teddy Sheringham kissed the ball in delight. I did not know what to do with myself as Klinsmann shaped up to take the penalty. My hands finally rested on my face as though I was praying. Klinsmann calmly slotted the ball into the bottom corner and the Spurs stand went crazy with a release of pent-up energy. We were jumping around, not knowing where to look. "Yesssssssss!" I partially lost my voice. We were back in it. The fans really got behind the team at this point as they sensed more goals were possible.

We were urging the players on until, to our dismay, Everton scored a third. It suddenly went very quiet. Ian Walker cried; I felt like it; others did. I still had distant hopes of forcing extra time but deep down I knew that this match would soon become the biggest disappointment of my Spurs-supporting life. The occasional song after this was in frustration. The fans could not be blamed for giving up. We had tried our hardest to support the team to victory, but the players were just not up to it on the day. They were supposedly the best team out there, with the better players, but Everton were hungrier, were first to every ball and completely outplayed Tottenham. The expectation had clearly got to the Spurs players. If the excuse last week against Southampton was that they were thinking of this game, they obviously were not thinking hard enough.

A few minutes before the end, Everton got their fourth goal. At this, I stood up, rammed my seat back and left (not normally something I ever do before the final whistle), as did many others. I was angry that my big day had been ruined. Some supporters stayed in their seats, a few crying, after the final whistle, stunned and wondering what had gone wrong. As we walked back to the coach, we heard the distant roar of the Everton fans as the final whistle must have gone.

Gary Mabbutt admitted afterwards that it was the worst performance since Gerry Francis had taken over. Why did they have to save it for that day? The whole team played badly. In terms of the atmosphere and the occasion it was the best match I had ever been to by a long way, but in terms of the result it was the worst by far.

I could not stop thinking about it the next day. I was supposed to be revising for my GCSEs but I could not concentrate. I obviously wanted to torture myself, re-live the feelings of despair I had experienced the day before, as I watched the whole game on video. As ever, it was just a case of having to wait a few days before I had recovered from the defeat. The idea of time being a healer holds true in the life of a football supporter.

There was still a month of the season remaining, though, and Spurs had a chance of qualifying for Europe through their league position. Only two days after the semi final defeat, Spurs played Manchester City at home. I was not sure how the players or the fans would react. The players would be shattered, physically and emotionally, but they probably wanted to show what they could do after their lacklustre display at the weekend. This indeed was the case, and Manchester City were subjected to the full force of a Tottenham vengeance as we dominated the first half. I could not believe it when City then took the lead just after half time. I thought the team might then crumble but the fans came to life and got right behind the team. We had been quiet despite the good first half, but it was like a new set of fans had turned up for the second half. Spurs were only behind for five minutes when David Howells scored a well-worked equaliser. The team were back to their best and the City goal had not broken their stride at all. If only they could have played like this two days previously, I would have been looking forward to an FA Cup final.

Klinsmann scored a thoroughly deserved winner with five minutes to go. Spurs had shown what they were really like, the performance and recovery extraordinary. It was a vital win, which we needed in our pursuit of a European place. Klinsmann had started to attract offers from other clubs for next season, and playing in European competition was imperative if we were going to keep him.

The importance of keeping Jurgen was underlined in the next game, away at Crystal Palace. Spurs did not put in a great performance, and some of the play was reminiscent of the semi final. I was beginning to think that the Manchester City game was a one-off and that the rest of the season would fall away. Spurs were losing 1-0 with five minutes to go, when we were awarded a free kick 25 yards out. Up stepped Jurgen. He did not usually take goal-scoring opportunity free kicks but he placed the ball with determination and intent. He then proceeded to bend the ball with power into the top corner. It was a superb strike and unlike any of his other goals that season. Amidst the celebration, the man sat next to me turned to face me and we both yelled "yesssssss", fists clenched. It was still a bad result, but, as a football fan, you go to games to witness such moments of genius.

A few days later we beat Norwich 1-0 at home in an uneventful contest. The game was only notable for the introduction of the giant television screen above the Park Lane stand. In an interview shown on the screen before the game, Jurgen joked that referees would now be able to see the penalty decisions that should have been given to him.

Wonderfully, Arsenal were having a poor season. At the end of the Crystal Palace match, we were singing "you're going down with the Arsenal", although I would never actually want the north London derby games to be missing from the fixture list. Realistically, Arsenal were not going to be relegated but, more importantly, Spurs stood a good chance of getting a result at Highbury at the end of April.

Not being season ticket holders meant that we could not get tickets for the game. Instead we went to a live screening on the big screen at

White Hart Lane. This was the first away match shown live after the installation of the screen. The whole Paxton Road end was full, and there were more fans there than either I or Spurs expected. I also did not really think there would be an atmosphere: what is the use in cheering and singing if the team cannot hear you? It was a north London derby though, and there was the unity of several thousand Spurs fans together. Indeed, there was actually a more intense atmosphere than at many home matches. I too found myself singing and shouting at the screen. It was a slightly surreal experience.

The match ended 1-1, Klinsmann scoring the equaliser. The goal was celebrated as though all the fans were at Highbury, with everyone jumping around, hugging each other.

Some Arsenal fans had come to watch the game at the Lane, either because they could not get tickets at Highbury or because they fancied causing some trouble. When Ian Wright scored, around ten or so, ridiculously outnumbered and not segregated, jumped up and cheered. A fight ensued and there was a rather comical sight of Spurs fans chasing Arsenal fans round the East Stand. Nobody was seriously injured, at least that I saw anyway. It was lucky more Arsenal fans had not decided to come to White Hart Lane that day. I think the club certainly had not anticipated it because there would not have been enough stewards or police to deal with a bigger disturbance.

Ian Wright furthered the feelings of hatred among Spurs fans for him that day. He fell easily in the box and won a penalty, from which he scored the opening goal, and swung an arm at Gary Mabbutt. The Spurs fans were incensed by this, Wright having clearly punched David Howells in the face off the ball in a game a couple of years previously. Spurs also had a 'goal' disallowed for offside, which proved an incorrect decision from the television replays. So this match could, maybe should, have been a 2-0 win, a result that would have increased our chances of qualifying for Europe no end.

The first Saturday in May saw Spurs play their second consecutive away London derby, against Queens Park Rangers. It was a hot, sunny spring afternoon. Unfortunately, that turned out to be the best thing about the day. A 2-1 loss meant that Spurs could no longer qualify for Europe. Furthermore, they were guaranteed a 7th place finish, unable to overtake or be caught by another team. A respectable league finish, given the poor start to the season. Some people are never happy though, and I heard one woman complaining after the match that the team and the manager were no good, that they were struggling. Seventh place and an FA Cup semi final was not a bad season, especially by Tottenham's standards. Thankfully she seemed in the minority, and it was probably an instant reaction to the loss anyway.

The worst, however, was still to come that day: Klinsmann gave the biggest indication yet that he would be leaving at the end of the season. Throughout the game, the focus of the singing was pleading with Jurgen to stay at Spurs. "Jurgen, stay another year." "Don't go Jurgen, don't go." He acknowledged this personal support at the end of the game. Like we had been doing for many weeks, we waited outside the players' entrance after the game in the hope of getting some players' autographs. All season, the one autograph we had been chasing above all others was Klinsmann's, but he was the one player who never ever stopped outside the ground. Again at QPR, he was steamrollered onto the waiting team coach by three stewards. This time, though, he reappeared a couple of minutes later to see the fans. There was a huge surge and crush, with autograph books hopefully being thrust into the air. We finally had Jurgen's autograph, but was this a form of goodbye to the supporters who had been waiting all season?

The match at home to Coventry three days later was of no importance, although that was no excuse for the appalling display, lack of effort and 3-1 loss. This was the first football match where I sat by myself, the others not seeing the point of going, which was a little strange, but I felt comfortably at home surrounded by Spurs supporters. The main feature of the game was the continued 'keep Jurgen' campaign. This time the songs were accompanied with large banners in some sections of the crowd. Retaining the services of Jurgen was the only remaining goal for the fans that season. He again saluted the fans at the full time whistle.

Two days later I heard the dreadful news. Just as I remember the moment I heard Jurgen had joined Tottenham, I also remember where I was when it was announced that his stay in N17 was to be all too brief. I was at school. I just sat there, saying nothing and not moving. Jurgen would definitely be leaving at the end of the season. It was expected really seeing as he had not shown any indication in the past few weeks that he might stay. Even so, I was still upset. I later watched the news in more detail at home. He gave his reasons (wanting a better chance to end his career winning trophies) and said that the fans had been "wünderbar". I had been part of this and I did shed a tear or two at his comment. He had had such a great rapport with the fans all season, and he said how good the supporters had been. He also mentioned that the non-stop pleading at recent matches had made the decision to leave more difficult. It had almost worked, but fan power had lost to the lure of medals at Bayern Munich.

It might have been expected for the fans to turn against a deserting player, especially after such a short stay. Klinsmann was an exception to this rule, due partly to his success and partly to his relationship with the fans. He said he hoped for an emotional farewell in the final game of the season, at home to Leeds, and I was hoping that he would receive one. His rapport with the fans and his manner throughout the season had endeared him to so many people. I was hoping he would go out with a bang, scoring the winning goal with a spectacular strike, and celebrating with his trademark dive. I could not have had any bad feelings towards him because of everything he had done in that one season. He provided me, and everyone else at the Lane, with incredible excitement and left me with some great memories. He also gave me 29 goals to celebrate that season. He was rightly voted 1995 Footballer of the Year by the Football Writers' Association. He would be missed greatly as a player and as a character.

Jurgen got his big send off against Leeds and was captain for the day, although there was no goal to complete a fairytale season. He came out on to the pitch to a standing ovation from all four sides of the ground, and he turned to wave to each in turn. The tune "walking in a Klinsmann wonderland" was sung repeatedly, as it had been all season. On one occasion, when he was in the six-yard box right in front of us, a loud rendition of the song started up among the section of fans around us. He waved and we cheered.

As is customary at the last home game of the season, there was a lap of honour after the match. Led by Jurgen, the players walked round the edge of the pitch, taking the applause of the fans and applauding them in return. When Jurgen came to face us, I held my hands particularly high to applaud just him. It was just him I watched as I felt he deserved my full attention and I hoped he would somehow see me in the crowd, but of course he would not. Goodbye and good luck, as said one banner.

The game itself finished 1-1, giving Leeds the point they needed to get into Europe. The biggest cheers from the Leeds fans, however, came when they heard Shearer had put Blackburn ahead in their vital title-chasing game against Liverpool, and then at the final whistle, when they learned their big rivals Manchester United had lost out to Blackburn in the race for the championship. It was as though they were Blackburn fans: they went mad, jumping around and shouting. They seemed to care more about their rivals losing the League than their own team gaining a place in Europe. It seemed strange to me then, and still does now. Unless it had a direct bearing on Tottenham's fortunes, I would never support another team more vigorously than my own.

As well as the focus rightly being on Klinsmann, there was much joy shown from the Spurs fans regarding our former midfielder Nayim's outrageous last minute winner from 50 yards out against Arsenal in the European Cup Winner's Cup final earlier in the week. "Nayim from the half-way line" was the cry, to the same tune as "1-0 to the Arsenal", their famous song all season.

So closed my first full, and proper, season of supporting Spurs. It had been so eventful, with exciting highs and disappointing lows. I had loved every kick of it though. I was properly hooked now and could not wait for the new campaign to begin. We had made the decision to upgrade from club members to season ticket holders, guaranteeing us a ticket for all home games, and virtually any away game, including a cup final should there be one. Would the summer produce another surprise and Spurs sign a high profile replacement for Klinsmann? This will sound strange, but at the end of the season I thought to myself that with my GCSE exams looming I would have something to occupy my time and keep my mind off football for much of the football-empty summer. Roll on August.

4. The season ticket years

In 1995, Tottenham and Arsenal were at roughly the same level. The gulf between the two sides has been embarrassingly large for much of the time since. The tide turned when, in the summer of 1995, Tottenham's big signing to replace Klinsmann was Chris Armstrong from Crystal Palace. At the same time, Arsenal brought Dennis Bergkamp to Highbury, and as Spurs remained at the same mediocre level, Arsenal started their rise to an entirely new one. Unfortunately, the optimistic terrace lyric of "we all agree Armstrong's better than Bergkamp" did not quite turn out to be true. The appointment of Arsene Wenger as Arsenal's manager a year later was the final catalyst for years of Arsenal success. I am still waiting for the tide to turn back in the other direction.

Arsenal managed to win the League not long after Bergkamp and Wenger's arrival. They became Champions due, in the main, to Dennis Bergkamp and a very tactically astute manager who spent his money extremely wisely, picking up relatively unknown players for small fees and grooming them into worldwide superstars. The prime example of this is Patrick Vieira, signed for a relative bargain at £3.5 million, who went on to become the club's captain and one of the best midfielders in the world. Arsenal have enjoyed many years of success with this formula, and it is only as I have been writing this book that any remote signs of slight deterioration have been evident. I suspect this is due in no small part to the departure of Vieira to Juventus and Bergkamp's retirement from his imperious career. It remains to be seen how much of an effect Thierry Henry's departure will have. Nevertheless, they have now developed a wealth of talented young players, from which their next great team will probably grow.

I do not begrudge any team being successful in the way Arsenal have done, even though it may grate to admit that. I believe there are two ways to win the League: through the appointment of the right manager, like Wenger at Arsenal and Ferguson at Manchester United, or through massive financial backing, like Blackburn Rovers and, especially, Chelsea. Manchester United's success was built on the back of giving the right manager time to establish himself and develop youth talent, while at the same time bringing the right signings to the club. Only through building this success were United able to accumulate the wealth that enabled them to make big money signings like Rio Ferdinand, Ruud van Nistolrooy and Wayne Rooney. United's wealth came about as a direct cause of their success and it has enabled them to remain as one of the top two sides in the country for over ten years (and counting).

Blackburn Rovers were the first team to win the League purely due to massive financial investment in a short period of time, but their stay at the top was a very short one and they have done nothing of note since finishing top of the pile in 1995. They, in fact, were relegated only four years after becoming Champions.

In the last few years, Chelsea have gatecrashed Arsenal's and Manchester United's party at the top of the table. They had been progressing extremely well since the late nineties, especially when you consider where they were at the beginning of that decade. By the turn of the Millennium they had assembled a good squad, which with the right manager and a little patience might well have seriously challenged the top two anyway. However, the ultimate reason for Chelsea's current success has been the investment from Roman Abramovich since 2003. I realise the players have to play well and the manager needs to get the tactics, team composition and training right, but they have basically bought English football's top prize, and it is this method of winning the League that I begrudge. The wealth gap between Chelsea and the rest is bigger than it has ever been between any clubs before. Chelsea were able to attract Mourinho after Abramovich's money had bought many top quality players to the club and there was the further prospect of a blank cheque book. They then had a top manager.

Chelsea's success is not based on an innovative playing system or assembling a carefully selected squad over time. The key to their success is to buy some of the best players in the world at over-inflated prices, attracting them with immense salaries. The nineteen other clubs in the league have no means of generating the necessary wealth to match them at their own game. Their artificially created success is likely to be self-perpetuating as they take the lion's share of all the prize money and TV rights. Achieving continual success through building a team and playing system over time with the perfect manager is somewhat more sporting. I will happily admit that I am jealous of Arsenal's and Manchester United's success; I would love Tottenham to be in their position. Although I would like to be in Chelsea's league position, I am not jealous of them or their fans. I can honestly say I would not want a billionaire to pump endless money into Tottenham Hotspur Football Club, even if it led to a quick Premiership title. I would probably enjoy the moment but it would be tainted with the fact that success had not been brought about by true sporting values. I would not want to be chanting the name of the chairman when my club had just won the League; I would want to be singing the names of the players and manager.

Can luck win the League? It is unlikely over 38 games that luck can play a sufficiently big part. It can win a cup competition, but not the League. Nevertheless, it is currently the only hope that Spurs have and at the start of each season I hope for a never-seen-before run of luck that will see Spurs storm to the top of the Premiership and keep the momentum going all year. It has not happened yet though, and I am not holding my breath.

I do believe that Spurs may now just have one vital ingredient of a successful club in Martin Jol, the manager since November 2004. He has built a young team of promising international players, some of whom have the potential to be stars in the future, and instructing them to play a mostly attractive passing game. Maybe, with time and patience, this team can challenge the top, just as Arsenal did in the mid to late 1990s. The biggest obstacle at the moment is Chelsea's billions.

Full of enthusiasm and excitement following the sensational (if not ultimately successful) spectre of that last Klinsmann-inspired season, I looked forward to the following August with huge eagerness. The 1995-96 season was the first of my two years as a Paxton Road season ticket holder. I attended 31 out of 38 league games home and away, as well as a further 5 cup games, the most matches I have been to in a season. It is virtually certain that I will never go to anywhere near as many in one year again.

As new season ticket holders we were invited to go to White Hart Lane during the summer and choose our seats in the empty stadium. It was quite a surreal experience, being in the ground, virtually alone with no football taking place. Despite the lack of matches, the summer close season still provides excitement and interest for the avid football fan. First, there's the all the speculation in the transfer market, which is especially rife when it comes to Spurs, and the prospect of new summer signings, although surely the arrival Klinsmann could not be bettered. There is usually also at least one new kit released (which is more exciting for some than others). Finally, only a month or so after each season ends, the fixtures for the new season are announced, meaning you can start planning your match-going. Choosing our regular seats that summer was another such way of keeping involved during the barren summer months.

The first two home games of the season were against Aston Villa and then Liverpool three days later. Unfortunately, it looked as though the departures of Klinsmann and Nick Barmby, our England international attacking midfielder, had taken their toll. Spurs lost both games, a John Barnes own goal the only time we hit the net. Klinsmann's replacement, Chris Armstrong, was finding it difficult settling in and did not look to have the quality needed to form a prolific partnership with Teddy Sheringham. Had the disallowed effort he put in the net against Villa counted, it may well have boosted his confidence right at the beginning of the season.

Tottenham were completely outplayed by Liverpool. We had no answer to their passing and movement and they scored a quite brilliant third goal after one particularly incisive move. The disillusionment was evident throughout the Spurs following: with no goals of our own to cheer, one supporter stood up to applaud the Liverpool goal, shouting "brilliant goal, well done". When the Liverpool fans sang "you're crap and you know you are" all we could do was applaud in agreement. There was no evidence to dispute it.

The first away match of the season was at West Ham. Another poor performance ended in a 1-1 draw. It was good to get to an away London derby early in the season. We were sat right next to the West Ham fans, which made the atmosphere and banter all the more enjoyable. One rendition of "Nayim from the half-way line" was silenced by Don Hutchison scoring the opening goal from 30 yards out. The West Ham fans' response was the inevitable but instant: "West Ham from the half-way line". Football fans can be surprisingly quick witted sometimes.

After this disappointing start to the season, I began to question how much I enjoyed this torturous hobby of mine. Why did I put myself through it? Even when Rosenthal scored the equaliser against West Ham, my celebration was more subdued than it had been the previous season. Maybe I was mourning Klinsmann's loss more than I thought. These doubts were quickly dispelled, however, as the team and the season really got going in the coming weeks.

Tottenham's and my season started at home to Leeds ten days after the visit to Upton Park. A much better team performance led to a 2-1 victory. Darren Anderton returned after injury, providing some much needed impetus, and Armstrong seemed to be slowly developing an understanding with Sheringham. For some reason, I spent the match sat in front of my friends. It must have been just how the tickets worked out. As a slightly insecure teenager, I found myself feeling self-conscious for large parts of the game as they could always see what I was doing, how I was singing and how I celebrated the goals. I felt as though I had to do everything 'correctly' and behave as they would, rather than just being myself. As a consequence, my reaction to our first goal was again a little subdued, and later, trying to impress left me feeling rather silly at one point. Brian Deane, the Leeds striker, pushing Dean Austin, our right full-back, off the ball prompted me to stand and shout abuse at the Leeds player. Unfortunately no-one else noticed and I was left standing on my own. I sat down quickly.

I managed to escape my self-consciousness, however, when the winner went in. A combination of factors meant that the goal was too important to worry about how I was looking to the others. The goal was at our end of the ground and we were sat right in line with the ball and the net. You could follow the ball from when it left Sheringham's boot to when it hit the net. It seemed to travel in slow motion. When you can see the line of the ball travelling into the goal, there is a split second before it hits the net when your heart stops; you know it is going to go in just before most people in the stadium do, and you are on your feet as the ball crosses the line. It was also a late winner, sealing the first win I had witnessed that season. A goal always seems to mean more, too, if there have been some controversial incidents and a good atmosphere to get the adrenalin flowing. I let my emotions out in full view of my three friends behind me.

Des Walker was already a Spurs favourite before our away trip to Sheffield Wednesday. He has never played for the club but his winning own goal in the 1991 FA Cup Final has put him in the Tottenham history books. An excellent defender, he was often greeted by the supporters' chant of "you'll never beat Des Walker" when he successfully beat his opponent. In this game, though, he again seemed to think he was playing for Tottenham.

He scored another own goal and gave away a penalty from which we scored in a 3-1 win. So again, we would not have won without him. The difference between the sides once more.

This was my first trip of the season outside London and it culminated in a well-deserved first win I had seen outside the capital. The old style stand we were in with its low roof meant that the noise from the away fans seemed louder than usual. Being in good voice with your fellow supporters can often be more enjoyable than the goals themselves. Even at 1-0 down our loyal fans stood to sing the team into action. There were rumblings of songs from the start about Walker's cup final effort, but only from isolated pockets of supporters. After his telling contribution in this game we cheered him and sung his name as though he were one of our own. Walker's contribution to the game (given the background) was quite comical and if any other Wednesday player made an error we all enquired "are you Walker in disguise?" The long coach journey home was filled, as usual, by Spurs videos. Of course one of the goals shown was that cup final own goal.

I realised during the journey home, perhaps due to enduring thoughts of our last FA Cup final victory, that I had never been to a winning game where the goals were so important that I imagine you would not know what to do with yourself when they went in due to the overdose of adrenalin and excitement pouring through you, where the joy overwhelmed you. I had never been to an FA Cup final, or even a winning semi final, or a game like the quarter final at Anfield a year previously or a big European game or a match to decide the title. I still have not either, not really. I support Spurs; games of that level do not come round that regularly. Sure, I have experienced moments that have made me extremely happy, breathless and overly-emotional. I have been to FA Cup semi finals, losing each time, numerous north London derbies, a winning League Cup semi final and final, but none of these are quite up there with the sport's highest levels of achievement and importance.

Chris Armstrong got his first goals for Spurs in a 4-0 win over Chester City in the League Cup. It was a very professional performance against a well-supported team who were top of their division. He was obviously relieved and the Spurs fans sung his name all night. In fact, the Spurs faithful had been extremely supportive of him all season, appreciating his hard-working performances, but we were willing him to get off the mark. We had sung his name as he left the pitch at Sheffield Wednesday, rather than the two-goal Teddy Sheringham.

Bergkamp on the other hand was having a hard time of it at Arsenal. He had not settled and was starting to get stick from their supporters. Ronny Rosenthal scored our fourth goal that night, poking in from four yards. The goal put him two ahead of Bergkamp for the season. How Armstrong's and Bergkamp's futures changed over the coming seasons.

QPR v Spurs on the evening of 25th September 1995 epitomised how 90 minutes of football can turn from total depression to being absolutely wonderfully amazing for a supporter. Thirty seconds into the second half Rangers scored to go 2-0 ahead; we were playing awfully. Nevertheless, attacking the Spurs support, we managed to get back into it through a penalty and a few minutes later Jason Dozzell pulled it back to 2-2. I could not believe it and we certainly did not deserve it. I went mad celebrating but more was to come: 50 seconds later Teddy Sheringham headed us in front. I can still see the ball hitting the net now. It was almost right in front of us. 2-1 down to 3-2 up in less than two minutes. The whole stand erupted with a noise I had not heard before. Every supporter was jumping around, going crazy, including me. I really could not believe this. Everybody was hugging each other and I turned to the people behind me as they almost fell on top of me. There was me and a bloke I had never met before roaring with clenched fists at each other, our faces a foot apart. I was so out of breath after this minute of partying that when I tried to join in with a song, it was not possible. I had to have a little rest. I had never myself or seen anyone else celebrate like that at a match I had been to by that time. According to various Spurs fanzines, the goal that sparked the wildest celebrations from Spurs fans in recent years was, unsurprisingly, Gazza's free kick against Arsenal in that 1991 FA Cup semi final. How good it would have been to be there. After I had regained my breath, I joined in with the non-stop singing that spilled out of the Spurs end for the rest of the match. My throat was so hoarse by the end, my voice almost lost.

Spurred on by that rousing comeback, we completely outplayed Wimbledon at home five days later. Sheringham had a classy game, scoring two goals. The fans sang "are you watching, Venables?", referring to the fact that the then England manager would be picking his squad soon. The goal celebrations were not quite as hectic as at QPR; they more reflected a general appreciation of an excellent footballing display. I felt I wanted to be jumping around but it did not feel natural to. I guess that sort of reaction is only natural for special or important goals, but defining those types of goals is not that straightforward; there are so many factors. The victory meant we were only three points off second place and well positioned to challenge for a European place. Even back then I dreamed of Tottenham winning the League.

There was a buzz around the stadium before our next home game, an air of expectation following our recent wins. Unfortunately, in typical Spurs fashion, any thoughts of grandeur were brought crashing to the ground with an appalling display and 1-0 loss to Nottingham Forest. I do not think we had one shot on goal.

It was around this time that I started to want to extend my social life beyond football. I was sixteen and had just started the sixth form college at my school. People were starting to go out on a Friday and Saturday night to parties and pubs. My problem was that I was not naturally part of one group of friends who were going out together at the weekends. Sure, I knew loads of people at school, people I would call friends, but my main social activity was the football.

By the October, it was starting to get me down. It seemed so important at the time to get in properly with this crowd so I could feel part of a group of friends and be someone who would be automatically invited out. I wanted to be able to get involved in the conversations that would take place during the week about the antics of the previous weekend.

I felt as though I was not cool enough and, even worse, did not really have many friends; it really started to depress me. It reached the point where I wrote on a piece of paper "I hate myself and my life." An overreaction probably but it was how I felt at the time. My Mum saw my message, and in all honesty I had left it out deliberately on show hoping that one of my parents would read it and be able to talk to me and reassure me.

With all these thoughts running round my head continuously, I was really looking forward to an away trip to Everton on 22nd October. I could not persuade anyone else to come so the game was to be not only my first away match outside London on my own, but my first ever match of any kind on my own. The only exceptions were some non-league matches at my local team Hampton FC. It was hardly daunting travelling five minutes to stand on an empty terrace though. Doing my paper round one morning in the week before the game I remember thinking how much I was looking forward to escaping for a day, immersing myself in my one social activity, one that I loved, even if I was going to be by myself. For that one day at least I would have an identity and belonging.

The result of the match was almost of secondary importance, but I did want some revenge for our FA Cup semi final drubbing the previous season. Surprisingly, the Everton fans sang about that game very little. They did, however, pick on Armstrong's relative failings so far that season. It backfired, though, as just as they were singing "what a waste of money", Armstrong lobbed their goalkeeper from 30 yards. A brilliant goal and the Spurs fans erupted around me; even the radio commentator commented on the fans' celebration apparently. We retorted with exactly the same words, only with a sarcastic tone. Everton equalised and the game deservedly ended 1-1, although we did have chances to win it, notably through Sheringham heading just wide and Rosenthal scuffing a shot that narrowly missed the corner flag from 12 yards out.

I eventually got back home at 1:30am, having been out for 18 hours. Some might say this is madness. I enjoyed it and it had served its ulterior purpose as well.

Following a 1-1 draw with league leaders Newcastle at home was another away trip, this time to Coventry and this time there were four of us. Spurs won 3-2, Sheringham again performing sublimely. My second north London derby was looming on the horizon and just how important this fixture is to Spurs fans was demonstrated by the chant "two weeks 'till Arsenal, there's only two weeks 'till Arsenal".

It is the biggest league game of the season for Spurs fans and I looked forward to it for the fortnight after the Coventry match. I was hoping for a repeat of the previous season's fixture.

There was the usual enhanced atmosphere before the match and much singing prior to kick off. After the toss, the teams swapped ends and David Seaman ran towards us. The tradition of applauding the opposition goalkeeper as he approaches his goal is naturally abandoned for the Arsenal game. With the memories of Nayim's audacious winner in the previous season's European Cup Winners' Cup final still fresh in the minds of Spurs fans, the whole of the Paxton Road end stood up and sang "Nayim from the half way line" whilst pointing at Seaman for about half a minute. It was probably quite intimidating.

This happened a lot during the game and at one point vast Spurs ranks stood and chanted "Nayeeeeeem" whilst bowing; this spread to the East Stand and then to the Park Lane end. With about two minutes to go it was sung just to rub salt in the wounds created by our impending 2-1 victory.

I enjoyed this win more than the previous year's; I think I savoured this one more and coming from a goal down to beat Arsenal has something special about it (mainly because it does not happen too often these days). When Spurs equalised, with everybody going crazy, the bloke behind me virtually fell on top of me. The game was the biggest of the day in the Premier League and later that evening I watched myself on Match of the Day celebrating, looking very happy with a big smile on my face, jumping up and down and punching the air. As the second and winning goal went in I was lost briefly in the people behind me.

At the end of the game, the whole Paxton Road end was jumping up and down singing "Tottenham, Tottenham, Tottenham …". I later saw this joy too on Match of the Day. Supporters in the Park Lane end later confirmed how the Paxton Road fans were going mad at the final whistle.

The singing continued on our exit from the ground, something only reserved for really very special victories. I had now seen two derby wins out of two.

Before the game we had seen the Arsenal coach making its way to the ground. Some of us were, shall we say, gesticulating up towards the windows and the Arsenal players' faces inside. James made one particular sign in the direction of their striker John Hartson; the hostile reception the coach was receiving was evidenced on his face as he did not look as though he was particularly looking forward to the game. Unfortunately, a police officer saw James's gesture and came over.

"Do you want to see the game?", he enquired.

"Sorry" was the sufficient reply. The threat of missing the match meant the apology was heartfelt enough for the officer.

We also encountered a spot of trouble on our way home. As our tube started pulling away from Seven Sisters station, two Arsenal fans walked past the window, giving us a variety of fingered salutes. James retaliated with a provocative 2-1 sign, causing one Arsenal fan to head butt the window and the other to punch it. I was just glad the tube continued speedily on its journey into the underground.

A week later Spurs were unable to make it back-to-back victories over my most hated teams. A drab 0-0 draw away to Chelsea, at a time when league positions would have suggested Tottenham should beat the Stamford Bridge team, was not even compensated for by a good atmosphere. The occasion was most memorable for the presence of police dogs on the pitch at half time, a sign of the mutual hatred between the two sets of supporters.

A second consecutive 0-0, at home to Everton, and a dull 1-0 win over QPR, the only goal being scored after three minutes, would not have been memorable occasions for 99 per cent of supporters present. For me, though, those two weekends in December signalled a big change in my life.

Since my low point in October, I had been more proactive in my efforts to acquire a social life outside football. Through a friend, more an acquaintance really, I knew from a friend of my brother's, I managed to basically invite myself to a house party I had heard about. It was an open house anyway and my request was greeted positively. I knew a few people going from school.

I did not know the host though. In such a situation you would have expected me to turn up a little late, after some people I might know would have had the chance to arrive. Not me. I was in London for the Everton game and the party was on a different train line to the one I used to get home. To save myself going home and then trying to get to the party, I decided to jump on the train out of Waterloo after the football and go straight to the party. This, of course, meant I got there very early, even before the party was supposed to start. Very excited at going to this, my first proper 'grown-up' party, I was greeted at the front door by the host in a towel. Susie was obviously not quite ready for any guests and did not know who the hell I was. Once I had introduced myself and explained that I was here to enjoy her hospitality for the evening, she let me in. She was a very friendly girl and happily chatted away to me as she invited me up to her bedroom. Only because there were no other guests there yet, naturally. I duly followed. After a couple of minutes of finding out if we had any mutual friends and so on, she said she needed to get dressed. Fair enough, I thought, and I obviously offered to go downstairs to have a beer and leave her to it.

"There's no need", she said.

Some people would have seen this as an invitation to stay, some as her just being too nice to ask me to leave. A mixture of my shyness and honourability meant that I left her to get dressed alone.

The party was good and I now had an instant packed social life at the weekends: going to the football in the afternoons and parties and pubs in the evenings. Football always took priority though.

That first party established a trait in me that still lingers today: I am always early for everything. I think I want to be the first there so I do not miss anything. I am also extremely reluctant to be the first to leave.

As Christmas approached, Spurs were sitting in an unusually lofty league position. A 1-0 win away at Wimbledon ten days before Christmas put Spurs just two points behind second place. The performance was not pretty but they still won, a commonly stated sign of a championship winning side. Surely we could not achieve this, but we had just put together a run of five clean sheets in a row and we were in a good position. What do you have if you do not have hope?

As usual at Selhurst Park against Wimbledon, Spurs fans filled more than half the ground, ensuring the game almost felt as though it was at home. It made for a good atmosphere, too. As the final whistle was nearing, the score was 0-0 and I resorted, as I did sometimes, to trying to imagine a goal going in. For the first time it worked. Just as my mind had seen it, a cross from the right was headed in by Ruel Fox. Positive thinking at its best.

There is nothing better in football than celebrating a late winner. It really is a superb feeling, a mixture of pent up frustration and newly-found joy coupled with the relief that the other team has very little, if any, time to get back into the game. The seated crowd at Selhurst became a jumping melee.

At the full time whistle we were dancing on our seats singing "Jingle bells, jingle bells, jingle all the way, oh what fun it is to sing when Tottenham win away", a song reserved for successful away trips during the Christmas period.

Just as Tottenham fans were getting excited about our league position at Christmas, in true Spurs style the excitement was quashed by some dreadful results over the festive period. Two days before Christmas, at home to Bolton, Spurs went 2-0 up courtesy of Sheringham and Armstrong. The win could well have put us second. From this position Tottenham managed to concede twice and finish with a draw against a team who had not won an away point so far that season. It seemed as though the players mimicked the attitude of the fans, thinking that the game was won at 2-0.

My Dad offered to take me to Southampton for the Boxing Day game. It was the first time I had sat with him at a Spurs match for a few years, and I was worried about how to behave in terms of singing and celebrating. He had only seen me as a quiet and timid spectator, before I had really got involved in games properly. Would I be comfortable enough to behave as I normally did when I went to the football with my friends? As it turned out, I did not have to worry about singing, let alone celebrating. A drab 0-0 draw was played out in a depressed atmosphere. There was not a meaningful shot until the 85th minute and the fans were so quiet at one point that "sssshhhhhhh" whispered all around the Dell.

Spurs did have a goal disallowed when Armstrong headed the ball out of the Southampton 'keeper's hands and rolled it into the empty net. My reaction was a reflex one as I jumped up briefly from my seat; I knew then that I would have had to celebrate as normal. I had no choice.

Any thoughts of winning the League were quickly dispelled that Boxing Day. We just were not good enough against the poorer teams like Bolton and Southampton, unable to pick up the easy three points. There was no killer instinct and a lack of depth in the squad. Against Southampton, several injuries meant that the midfield in particular was very poor.

The day before New Year's Eve, I travelled away to Blackburn, the reigning League champions. I did the 400 mile plus round trip on the Spurs coaches by myself. Such journeys really are too long to spend by yourself. As I have said before though, it does feel like you are surrounded by friends, who, although may not be like minded people, all want the same outcome from the day.

My overriding memory from the match was how unbelievably cold it was inside Ewood Park. I had two pairs of socks on, tracksuit bottoms under my jeans, several layers of t-shirts and jumpers and a hat, scarf and gloves. Despite all this, I was still chilled to the bone by the biting wind that was blowing in from the rural area where the stadium was situated.

Up until the game, Spurs had an unusually enviable record away from home that season. They were so far unbeaten on their travels but the first away defeat came that day, Blackburn triumphing 2-1. In actual fact, Spurs were a little unlucky and probably deserved a draw. Their effort on such a cold day was recognised by the fans who stood to applaud them off the pitch at the final whistle. The support was good all round that day. People were standing up and singing when we were losing. That, and clapping the players off after a loss, does not happen to such a widespread extent at away matches further south and virtually never at home. There seems to be a feeling that if you have travelled all that way you want to see a win more, and will do what you can to aid that outcome.

As the new year dawned, I witnessed one of the best Spurs victories that I have ever been lucky enough to see. Eventual Premiership champions Manchester United were the visitors to White Hart Lane on New Year's Day.

We went to the pub beforehand to get in the mood. The singing had already started. The fans were up for this, sensing a good start to the new year would be vital in maintaining our league position that had looked like slipping away in recent games. Where better to get back on track than against Manchester United?

The atmosphere that started in the pub transferred to the stadium and carried on all through the evening. There was an air of excitement all night, due in part no doubt to the visit of a team such as United and, at least for me personally, the prospect of watching the team under the floodlights.

No matter how bad the current run of form is, over the years Spurs have nearly always managed to raise their game for the big teams, especially at home. Even I did not expect them to raise it as they did in this match though. A 2-1 half time lead turned into 4-1 by the final whistle courtesy of two goals from Chris Armstrong. We had thrashed Manchester United, who would go on to win the double that season; I could not quite believe the result, but it was thoroughly deserved on the night. Both clubs had about half their first team injured, although many commentators seem to remember only United having players out, as if to excuse the defeat. Tottenham played some scintillating stuff, which, coupled with the odd United mistake, meant that we were on top throughout. We looked like a team competing for the title.

At the final whistle the whole Paxton Road end was singing "Always look on the bright side of life", sarcastically mimicking the United fans who had used the song regularly when they won the title a couple of years previously.

A couple of weeks later Spurs played the other Manchester team, City, at home. The result was the same, but the score and manner of victory very different. A single Chris Armstrong goal earned us the victory that day. The game had nowhere near the excitement of the United game, but vitally the team ground out the result. It was deserved, their 'keeper making many saves throughout the course of the game.

There was one comical moment delivered by the City fans. To the tune of Oasis's hit Wonderwall, they sang their own rendition towards their manager with the words "… and after all, you are Alan Ball". Who says football fans do not have brains and wit?

The win meant we remained fourth in the league table. It was an unusual position to be in, but fans were still criticising the team, their expectations rising with every league place gained. I was having trouble myself admitting that Spurs might actually be pretty good for once.

Despite the previous season's tragic exit in the semi final of the FA Cup, the competition was still as popular as ever among the Spurs fans the following year. The third round draw had given Tottenham an away match at Hereford. Such is the supporters' special affection towards the competition, people apparently were queuing at 5.30am for tickets – to see Hereford.

I did not go to the original tie, which ended all square. I did, however, make it to the replay staged at White Hart Lane ten days later. The ground was very nearly full, again underlining the importance of the Cup among the fans. The atmosphere was good, with more songs than at a run of the mill home league game. It was an easy win in the end, Sheringham bagging a hatrick and Armstrong a brace.

As with the game against Altrincham in 1995, part of me wished to see Hereford score. I wanted to see their fans' reaction to a one-off goal against one of the top teams in the country. It duly arrived and they went mad. The Tottenham fans stood and clapped, probably rather patronisingly, at their achievement.

After a disappointing loss 2-1 away at Aston Villa, another team (as well as Chelsea) that we seemed to be cursed by at the time, the FA Cup returned quickly with a fourth round tie at home to Wolverhampton Wanderers. The better opposition, although still not Premiership standard, meant there was a proper cup atmosphere. The game was closer than expected, too. Spurs did not play well but importantly showed their superiority in the replay to progress to the next round. From a personal point of view, I was desperate to banish the memory of the previous season's semi final misery and go one step further this year. It was a case of so far, so good.

Spurs have an awful record at Anfield, so any kind of positive result there is greatly appreciated. The game itself is always special. It was less than twelve months since that historic FA Cup quarter final victory. A similar result on my first visit to the famous home of Liverpool Football Club would have been very welcome, just so I could have seen a glimpse of what that afternoon must have been like in the stands.

My brother Simon came with me that day and sat with me in the Spurs end. He is a Liverpool supporter purely because they were the class team when he first became interested in the game as a young boy. It must be very odd sitting with the away fans at your home ground, something I hope I never have to do, but he did not get to see too many live games and so jumped at the chance of accompanying me. He paid the Spurs fans the ultimate compliment, saying that the noise they made was "deafening".

Even on my first visit I appreciated what a special place Anfield was. I thought to myself that it was the best stadium I had ever been to. I have only been there a couple of times, but it is still my favourite away trip, better than going to Old Trafford. As You'll Never Walk Alone was played as the players entered the pitch and the whole Kop stood with scarves raised above their heads, I remember thinking what a magnificent sight this was, surely one of the best in world football. We tried our best to drown it out with songs of our own, but secretly I just wanted to listen to this football anthem and watch the colourful Kop some 100 metres away. I would have loved to have gone to Anfield when the Kop was still terracing; I am sure the experience would have been even better.

As Simon had said, the noise around us was loud and the atmosphere was lively throughout, fuelled by the occasion of playing at this great stadium and no doubt heightened further following the previous season's cup win.

The game ended 0-0 but it was far from dull. Both teams had chances and a draw was well deserved. Liverpool striker Robbie

Fowler came on the radio later saying he had been man of the match and that Spurs had come to defend. That was probably as blinkered a view as mine that Spurs had all the best chances.

Still, it was a positive performance and a good result, much appreciated by the fans who applauded the players off at the end and there were even some songs to accompany them down the tunnel. The singing was unusual for a draw but it showed how good the result was. Deep down, though, as I clapped the players off the pitch, I regretted not being there ten months earlier when the Anfield Road end would have been one big party, rather than simply contented.

Luckily, the nature of the FA Cup is that the next round comes around very quickly. I was looking forward to my seventeenth birthday with great eagerness. The fifth round tie, away at Nottingham Forest, was scheduled for the Wednesday evening of my birthday. As it was during half term I was able to go to the midweek fixture and I could not wait. After missing out on the celebrations away at Anfield, this had the potential to be the best match I had ever been to: a big away FA Cup tie, an evening game and on my birthday. They had to win for the last reason alone surely. I had not looked at the weather forecast though.

James and I got the coach up from Tottenham during the afternoon. It helped to build the excitement, being part of a convoy going up to Nottingham to hopefully witness a famous cup win. We arrived in plenty of time to get involved in the pre-match atmosphere, which was superb. The tension and anticipation meant the singing started well before kick off. I was sure those around me wanted to avenge last season's exit too.

It was a cold evening. Just before kick off a few flakes of snow started to fall. Nothing to worry about. The electrifying atmosphere continued as the game kicked off. The snow was getting heavier.

I do not remember much about the opening exchanges of the match, probably because not much happened in the first few minutes. It is all a bit hazy in two senses of the word, mainly because my memories are dominated by what happened next, but also because it literally was hazy. The snow had become really quite heavy and the players were starting to fade in the distance. I was getting worried. After fifteen minutes, I turned to look towards Ian Walker's goal at the far end of the pitch; I could not see beyond the half way line.

The match was abandoned a couple of minutes later, with visibility virtually nil. I had never seen such a blizzard. After a few moments wondering whether this really was all the football we were going to see that evening, an announcement was made, confirming that we should leave the stadium, and make our way back home.

The coaches returned down the M1 at 30 mph due to the weather full of dejected Spurs fans, myself included. I got back through my front door at 2.45am after seeing just a quarter of an hour of meaningless football. Happy birthday Olly! Memories of that Monaco game around my ninth birthday came flooding back.

I could not make the rearranged match as it was an evening game at Forest on a week night during term time. The game did, however, end in a draw, which meant I would get to see the replay at the Lane. Not all bad then; I could still get to witness a historic cup win.

Things started badly in the replay as Forest got an early goal. After half an hour, though, came the first personal highlight of the tie. Teddy Sheringham hit a superb thirty yard free kick right into the top corner.

I did not initially believe it had gone in and my celebration must have been delayed, but the stadium erupted. I remember that moment being one of the highlights of the season, and much of it was borne out of relief.

Cup ties of this calibre are quite spectacular events at White Hart Lane. A special cup atmosphere fills the stadium, the supporters full of hope and expectation of another historic cup run. Against Forest even the normally sedate West Stand inhabitants, renowned for little noise, were singing the Wembley songs. It was a good game too and Spurs had a host of chances they should have converted to win the game quite easily.

Spurs being Spurs, though, did not want to ease the fans' nerves and do it the easy way and so the match eventually went to a penalty shoot out, the first I had witnessed live at a game involving Tottenham. The cup tie had gone as far as it could have. We were sat right behind the goal where the penalties would be taken, just a few rows back; we had the best view in the stadium.

Still in goal for Forest was Mark Crossley, famous for that save from Gary Lineker's penalty in the 1991 FA Cup Final. Penalty shoot-outs are the most nerve-racking part of a football match; being there was ten times worse than watching on television. As it turned out, it was a horrible experience. Crossley saved three times, including from Sheringham, his last dive and save winning the tie for Forest. My last memory from the day is a slightly podgy Mark Crossley running the length of the pitch to the Forest fans.

The tie had been jinxed from start to finish. All my expectation and hope was replaced by pain and anguish. I was also beginning to think that I was starting to curse this once great FA Cup side with my presence at big cup ties. Little did I know that my bad FA Cup experiences had not even started yet; it would get a whole lot worse in years to come.

Among all the drama of these cup matches were a series of boring 1-0 league matches at home. The Forest games and these matches showed the whole range of boredom to excitement a football match can bring you, Forest at the top end and these three one-nils right at the bottom. There was a 1-0 loss to West Ham before the abandoned tie and two consecutive 1-0 victories over Sheffield Wednesday and Southampton before the replay.

I think both the players and the fans found it difficult to raise themselves for these league matches against run of the mill opposition when there was an exciting cup run on the horizon. I know I did not have my usual enthusiasm and there was a subdued atmosphere all around me, but we still expect professional players to be committed and combative no matter the game. Both the players and the fans were poor, though, and there were about as many shots as songs.

The cup run was over for another year but there was still a good league finish to push for. Spurs were sixth in the table at this stage and hopes remained of European qualification. The fashion in which we exited the FA Cup, however, seemed to sap all impetus from the rest of the season. We were out of both cups and began to slip down the league. There just was not the same excitement as the previous season, no Klinsmann factor.

A week after the Forest game it was back to league business and a game at home to Blackburn. The disappointment in the players was still apparent from the previous week and Blackburn took a two goal lead before half time. Both were courtesy of their star striker Alan Shearer, the first a penalty after an extremely debatable fall by the same player.

To their credit, though, and possibly due to an enormous kick up the backside at half time, the players came out fighting in the second half. The team suddenly had spirit that they had not had in the first half and they finally seemed determined to put the cup disappointment behind them.

First, Sheringham pulled one goal back and then Armstrong drove in an equaliser. Both goals were right in front of us, and the Paxton Road was happy once more, finally having something to cheer about. I felt a mixture of relief and pride at how the team had dug deep to draw level. There only looked like being one winner, too, as Spurs pressed forward for a third and decisive goal. As was the Tottenham way, however, after fighting so hard to get back in the game, they allowed Shearer to sneak behind the defence in injury time to claim his hatrick and a 3-2 win for Blackburn. It was agony to lose so late in the game after getting back to 2-2 in the second half; it was reminiscent of the Aston Villa 4-3 loss the previous season.

After seeing a fairly comfortable 3-1 win over Coventry at home, there was further Forest misery to come. I must have been a glutton for punishment. After the abandoned blizzard game and the penalty shoot out loss right in front of me, I decided I still wanted to go back to the City Ground in Nottingham for the league game in April. Maybe I thought the law of averages would be smiling on me; maybe I thought the players would want revenge as much as I did just a few weeks after the cup tie.

Apparently, the law of averages had never been to Nottingham, and many of the players played like they had not gone through the excruciating FA Cup exit. We were soundly beaten, the 2-1 scoreline flattering us. Our goal was a consolation, headed in by Armstrong when Forest were already leading 2-0.

And so I returned down the M1, disappointed once more. Still, at least there was no snow to slow our progress back home this time.

My season ended rather tamely with two non-descript 1-1 draws at home to Middlesbrough and then Chelsea, the latter further adding to the period since the last victory over the team from Stamford Bridge.

Tottenham ended up missing out on a European place on the last day of the season after a draw at Newcastle, which was further disappointment at the end of a long season for me personally. Nevertheless, Gerry Francis had led the team to an eighth place finish (and only two points behind Aston Villa in fourth place) to go with the seventh achieved the previous year. He had, therefore, been the most successful manager since Terry Venables guided a Lineker and Gascoigne inspired team to third place and the FA Cup triumph in consecutive seasons. Another plus point had been the partnership between Sheringham and Armstrong. The pair had scored 46 goals between them, despite Armstrong's slow start. This was in fact only five fewer than Sheringham and Klinsmann had managed together in their glittering season.

As the season drew to a close, stalwart and captain Gary Mabbutt signed a new two year contract. He said he thought we had a good squad and that Spurs had the potential to challenge for the League title the following season. He sounded about as blinkered by hope as I was. I wonder if he was serious; it was Spurs he was talking about after all.

Alas for Mabbutt, his unrealistic aspirations for the 1996/97 campaign were dashed (for him personally at least) 18 minutes into the season when he suffered a broken leg in the opening game at Blackburn. Unfortunately, it was really the beginning of the end for the club's greatest servant since I started supporting them. In fact, this injury was to set the scene for the next few months as the club seemed to have a never ending stream of players ending up on the treatment table. It was rather like a conveyor belt; just as one player recovered, others would get injured.

That season was my second and last as a season ticket holder. The others did not renew, unable to justify the increased expense of suddenly (and ridiculously) moving into the adult price band at the age of sixteen. Even though we were in full time education, we were now expected to pay the same as earning adults. Consequently, I spent much of the season going to games by myself. I did not make it to as many games as the previous season – 27 in total – and I remember comparatively little about it. In hindsight this no doubt reflects the level of excitement and success that the season brought.

Unusually for the always much-anticipated first home game of the season, there were some empty seats. The fans who stayed away may have got it right as the uninspiring 1-1 draw with Derby paved the way for what was to follow over the next nine months.

Luckily the match was briefly enlivened by one moment of magic from Sheringham that resulted in us taking the lead. From a free kick 25 yards out he flicked the ball up from a short pass and put an audacious volley just over the bar. He got another chance immediately as the referee decided the Derby players were not back ten yards. This time he settled for a more conventional, but no less spectacular, curled shot into the top corner to put us 1-0 ahead.

We should have gone on to seal the win, but in injury time Derby sneaked an equaliser. A lapse of concentration in the defence cost us dear.

I went to my first away game a couple of weeks later, although playing Wimbledon at Selhurst Park as usual felt like a home game given the level of support Spurs fans had compared with the home side. It was a poor game that Wimbledon ended up winning 1-0, scoring their first goal of the season to do so. There were several fiery incidents on the pitch that helped bring the match to life but we had started the season simply not playing well enough.

By mid-September I had actually been to more away games than home games. I missed a couple of matches at White Hart Lane but made the short trip down to Southampton. We spent much of the 90 minutes entertaining ourselves by singing about Ronny Rosenthal's cup hatrick in 1995. I got to see my first win of the season, too. Chris Armstrong converted a penalty after a Southampton defender had decided to play basketball with his cross.

I still felt I had not celebrated a goal properly in these first few weeks of the campaign, partly because I had only seen two of them so far and also because neither had hardly been what you would call 'big' goals.

Spurs had started the season poorly and the fans made their feelings known in the next home game, against Leicester, as boos followed the players off the pitch at full time after another defeat. Part of the blame, however, could be pointed at the long injury list we had been accumulating. Even though the season was only a few games old, the team had already had to do without Sheringham, Armstrong and Anderton (as well as Mabbutt) for short spells. Gerry Francis had so far been unable to put out his first eleven. He had to resort to playing central defender Sol Campbell up front against Leicester. Although he (rather luckily) won the penalty from which we scored our goal, his presence at the back was missed as Leicester scored twice to win the game.

Sol had broken into the first team over the previous couple of years. A strong centre-back, he quickly established himself in the starting eleven. He actually made his debut, coming off the bench in a game against Chelsea, as a striker. He scored within minutes. However, it was soon realised that he would be a greater asset to the team in defence, and although he did fill in sometimes in attack, it was in the centre of defence that he made his name. Indeed, it was not too long before he was made Tottenham captain and became a regular in the England team. He was a bit of an idol of mine, until he left of course.

Following a comfortable 3-0 win over Preston in the second round of the League Cup, watched by only 20,000 spectators, (something that would not happen now at the Lane given the stampeding demand for tickets), came the most interesting moment of the season so far, for me at least anyway.

On 12th October 1996, I saw my one hundredth Spurs game. Before the kick off, I was confident that this personal milestone would guarantee a victory. I was growing more and more disappointed, however, as a dull and goalless game was making its way uneventfully through the second half.

Eighteen months before this match, the Villa goalkeeper, Mark Bosnich, knocked Klinsmann unconscious with his legs in a clumsy challenge on the edge of the penalty area. Football fans never forget and the Spurs contingent were of course taunting him constantly as he stood in front of his goal at the Paxton Road end. I was not really joining in, instead concentrating more on the lack of a goal.

One can only speculate what made Bosnich decide to do what he did next. Presumably fed up with all the goading, he turned to face a stand full of Spurs fans, many of whom were proud of the Jewish history associated with the club, and gave a Nazi salute. He really cannot have thought this through and it nearly caused a small riot around me. Bosnich later claimed his act was a reference to the German, Klinsmann, and a bit of harmless banter. Whatever the reason, he should have stopped for a second to consider his action.

Something that cannot be denied is that the incident livened up a very dull game. I was getting worried that my hundredth game would not be marked with a win. Finally, my hopes and expectations were realised as our Danish midfielder Allan Nielsen tapped in following a goalmouth scramble. I am sure I must have been happier than most in the ground. In response to what had happened earlier, Sheringham seemed to take almost as much delight in the goal as me. He picked the ball out of the net and showed it to Bosnich before dropping it in front of him.

The win against Villa actually started a run of five wins in six matches. One of those was a 2-1 victory over Sunderland in the third round of the League Cup. For some reason I left the game early and missed the winning goal scored one minute from time by Sol Campbell. I heard the roar as I walked down Paxton Road. The difference of being a few more metres away from the pitch outside the ground meant that the celebration was nowhere near the same as would normally greet a last minute winner if you were sat behind the goal watching the ball go in.

Next up, a few days later, was Chelsea at Stamford Bridge. The game was overshadowed by the death a few days previously of Chelsea Vice Chairman, Matthew Harding, in a helicopter crash. It was an emotional day for Chelsea fans, with various tributes and flowers being laid. Unfortunately, the reported good nature supposedly shown by both sets of fans was not universally evident. There was a substantial amount of noise around me during the minute's silence, and, worse, some very distasteful songs about Harding's death. I understand as much as the next fan the extent of the rivalry that exists with Chelsea (indeed for me it is almost as fierce as with Arsenal), but I was ashamed to be part of a Spurs crowd, albeit a small minority, singing about a man's death that day.

I just wanted to concentrate on the game and it was the first time that season that I really got into it. The view from the back of the lower tier of the East Stand was dreadful. Every time people in the rows in front stood up, I would react in kind to try to see the game but then the pitch would be almost entirely obscured by the supporters below me and the middle tier of the stand above me. In between the heads and rafters was a thin green strip.

Despite my vantage point, I did manage to see Chris Armstrong's equaliser to Ruud Gullit's opener. The noise in my claustrophobic section of the stand reverberated off the roof a short distance above my head, and made for a very intense atmosphere as the goal was scored and in the minutes afterwards.

Any crazy hopes of going on to record a victory against Chelsea were dashed in the second half as Chelsea scored twice to put the usual slant on the scoreline between the two clubs.

Two routine home wins followed for me, the first over West Ham, courtesy of an Armstrong goal, and then a 2-0 win over Sunderland. Winger Andy Sinton scored a quite amazing first in this latter match. Receiving the ball tight on the touchline just inside Sunderland's half, he cut inside, beating a couple of defenders on his way to the penalty area. He then cutely dropped his shoulder, completely deceiving his advancing opponent, before comprehensively drilling the ball into the far corner from ten yards out.

Sheringham missed a penalty ten minutes from time and had started to get a bit of stick from the crowd. Luckily, he made amends with a goal at the death, deservedly silencing his critics.

I have only ever been to Highbury twice. The first was to see Arsenal play Liverpool for my brother's birthday and the other was for a north London derby. Away at Arsenal is the most in-demand game for Spurs fans every season. Only season ticket holders have a chance of getting a ticket, so I am glad I took advantage while I could.

I felt a little intimidated walking to the ground by myself from Arsenal tube station, dauntingly a sole Spurs fan among a sea of red in the streets. I looked out for fellow Tottenham supporters but they had mostly been sensible like me and either covered up or left their colours at home for the afternoon. In fact I was in a black suit as I had come straight from my Sunday job. Probably the smartest person, in the fashion sense, in the stadium. There was actually a bit of trouble before the game so I am glad I was not showing my allegiance in any way.

Unfortunately, my one and only away game at Highbury did not turn out the way I had hoped. Arsenal took the lead from a penalty converted by my least favourite person on the pitch, Ian Wright. The atmosphere was unique and incredibly thick in the pocket of the ground I was in as the early winter night grew dark. There was an entirely never say die attitude. The fans' perseverance eventually paid off. After several good chances to equalise we got a goal in a very fortunate manner. Andy Sinton's shot beat Lukic's dive and hit the post. It bounced back into play and struck the Arsenal goalkeeper's head, causing it to roll back into the net. The intensity in the Spurs end had been building all game and the goal caused a burst of energy and wild celebrations. I seem to remember standing for the majority of the remainder of the game.

I would have settled for a draw but in the last ten minutes Arsenal scored twice, first with an atypical Tony Adams volley and then an entirely typical Bergkamp masterpiece. Highbury went into raptures at this third goal. I was distraught, but despite the disappointment, an air of solidarity and pride remained around me. Arsenal away is a very tiring experience, physically and emotionally, footballing support intensity at its peak. I doubt I will get to go again.

Ten days later against Liverpool was a completely different experience. We lost 2-0 but in all honesty we could have conceded six again, just a few days after being knocked out of the League Cup by a 6-1 thrashing at Bolton.

The performance was not good and the boos returned. The team were not good enough but some fans really thought they were terrible.

Their way of letting the players know made me feel sad. No matter how frustrated you are with the way the team are playing, I fail to see how booing the team you support can have a positive impact. The solidarity that was evident throughout at Highbury seemed to have got lost somewhere on the Seven Sisters Road. I walked slowly back to White Hart Lane station after the game.

I felt it was so important to get a win after the Liverpool experience, both to prove the boo-boys wrong and make me feel happy again about supporting Spurs. Just five days later the perfect tonic arrived in an away game at Coventry. It was my first coach trip of the season.

Away from the pressures of a demanding home crowd, the team played some good football and deservedly went ahead through Teddy Sheringham after half an hour. We were really on top but for some reason could not add to our tally. Eventually, as so often happens with Spurs, Coventry equalised. We should have been comfortably ahead but were instead level. To the team's credit, however, they responded positively and with fifteen minutes to go Andy Sinton lofted the ball over the Coventry 'keeper and into the net. It turned out to be the winner. I personally was so happy we had managed to secure the win and I let out a big roar of relief, fists aloft, when Sinton scored his goal.

After seeing an unexciting 1-1 draw at home to Sheffield Wednesday four days before Christmas, and suffering the embarrassment, although luckily not in person, of a 7-1 mauling away at Newcastle, the FA Cup returned on the first weekend in January. We had been drawn away at Manchester United and I made sure I had my ticket. With the league displays so poor, the cup was a welcome distraction and something different to focus on, if only for a weekend.

I had to get a 5.30 train up to Waterloo to make sure I caught the coach from outside the ground. The large ticket allocation and lure of a big FA Cup tie meant there were tens of Spurs coaches making their way north. Upon arrival, for reasons best known to the authorities, we had to queue for two and half hours to get inside Old Trafford. It was a freezing January day and it was one of the coldest waits of my life.

The long injury list we had been plagued with all season was still full of first team players. Consequently, the side we put out was extremely young and had very little experience. Manchester United were undoubtedly favourites to win; it was almost as though we were lower league underdogs that day.

The thousands who had made the journey, however, were determined to enjoy the day and the atmosphere was spectacular. As the players entered the pitch, hundreds of blue and white balloons were thrown into the air and bounced around above us. Giant flags were passed above our heads. It must have been an encouraging and inspiring sight for our youthful team. We did not sit down once.

Our young players did us proud against United's superstars. At one point it looked as though we might be able to get a shock result. We held out until early in the second half when Paul Scholes scored. The fans were not deterred by going behind and several of us stood to start singing again; within seconds the Spurs end was in full voice once more. This match was one of the few times I had felt able to start songs by myself; usually it was a case of joining in, vociferously and whole-heartedly of course, but at this cup tie everyone was so eager to back the team.

The belief we had was almost justified at one point. One of our young strikers, Rory Allen, had a great chance to equalise but just missed the target. For all the effort, by the players and supporters, it was not going to be our day.

Our fate was sealed near the end as a trademark Beckham free kick sailed into the top corner. Still the supporters would not let it spoil the day. The reaction was unbelievable given that we had just gone 2-0 down. We were singing and cheering until the final whistle. It was the most enjoyable defeat I had ever been to.

Ian Walker, our goalkeeper, summed up the afternoon. He was clearly disappointed at being knocked out of the cup but spent an unusually long time in front of the Spurs fans applauding us, just as we applauded our team from the pitch, spirits hardly dampened and full of pride.

In actual fact, the home league fixture against United was the following week. It turned out to be a continuation of the cup game in many ways. There was a superb atmosphere for a home game and we were mightily unlucky too. The players seemed to take confidence from the cup game and we matched United completely this time. One main difference between the two games was that central defender, Ramon Vega, had joined the club in the intervening period. Unfortunately, he could not reverse our fortunes and he turned out to be a rather calamitous defender.

The scoreline was 2-1 to United this time, slightly closer, but another undeserved loss was hard to take. United striker, Solksjaer, opened the scoring for United only for Rory Allen to equalise. Our young Norwegian striker, Steffen Iversen, then hit the bar with a dipping 25 yard volley only for Sinton to do the same with the follow up. It was just not meant to be. The game was again decided by a wonderful Beckham goal. This time he picked the ball up in the middle of the Spurs half, advanced a little before unleashing an unstoppable shot into the top corner. It had been a traumatic couple of defeats but you could not have asked for any more effort from the players.

After a 2-1 win over Blackburn at home the next three games I saw were consecutively against Tottenham's three biggest rivals: Arsenal, Chelsea and West Ham. First up was Chelsea. I was now going into games with them believing we would not win. The blind hope most football fans immerse themselves in was just not there any more where this fixture was concerned. It was, therefore, of no surprise that Chelsea scored within a minute of the start. The usual routine was continuing and I knew from that moment that the frustrating run was not going to end that day. Roberto Di Matteo added a second with a screamer into the top corner. For the record, veteran midfielder David Howells scored our consolation.

After a tight game as usual at home to Arsenal, where despite the incredibly passionate crowd, no goals were scored by either team, I made the trip to Upton Park for what turned out to be the most thrilling of the three derbies. Sadly, the result did not go our way; it is depressing when you fail to see your team record a victory over each of your main rivals, one after the other. The West Ham match was one of those topsy-turvy games (that football fans both love and hate at the same time) where both sides were in front at different stages. I was gutted when Julian Dicks hammered in a winning penalty to make it 4-3 in the closing stages. It was a miserable afternoon weather-wise, something that reflected my mood after what I had seen in recent weeks.

Despite never giving up and performing as well as they probably could, the team were just unable to put some wins together, even in these biggest of games.

My season petered out after this. There was very little for the club to play for. To say I lost interest would be taking it too far but I did not go to games with the same passion and enthusiasm in the last few weeks of the season. As happens in most relationships, I guess I was going through a period of disillusionment. Deep down, though, you know the love is still there; it is just a matter of reigniting it. Consequently, I still went, hoping for an improvement or, failing that, some kind of memorable performance, goal or piece of skill as a one off, but always supporting the team proudly and whole-heartedly.

The same feelings I was having also seemed to be apparent among some of the players. After seeing a forgettable 1-0 loss to Forest and a 1-0 win over Leeds, I travelled to Derby. Never mind the fact that we lost 4-2, putting in another uninspiring performance, the most disappointing thing about the game was Sheringham's demeanour. He played and carried himself around the pitch with a similar lack of enthusiasm to mine. I knew then he wanted to leave. And why not? He must have wondered what he was doing playing in a team of this standard. He deserved to be in a side challenging for honours, not struggling through the last games of another mediocre season. Indeed, I was right; he left that summer to join Manchester United.

I did regain my keenness once more that season. After seeing a 1-0 win over Wimbledon and a 1-1 draw at Aston Villa, the penultimate game of the season, at home to Middlesbrough on 25th April, fell exactly ten years to the day since my first at Tottenham. It was a fairly meaningless match to most in the stadium, but I desperately wanted to see a win, and I was sure the omens would ensure the right result. Because of this, I must have been happier than nearly everyone else around me when Andy Sinton bundled the ball home for the only goal of the game, my jubilant celebrations not befitting the low importance of the goal in the grand scheme of things. A decade apart I had seen my beloved Tottenham Hotspur win on each occasion, and I knew that my recent lack of interest was only temporary, much like many relationships I imagine.

The season still ended on a bad note, though. We lost 2-1 at home to Coventry and went 2-0 behind at one stage. It was a disappointing end to the season; you always want to sign off for the summer in a positive way, as I am sure the players do. The squad did their usual lap of honour after the game but early cup exits and an unexciting league campaign meant there was little to celebrate. The manager, Gerry Francis, summed it up perfectly when he said the season had been "a total write off".

And so ended the last of four seasons where I had been going to the majority of games. Football had been my primary focus and I had very few other interests and pressures during this period. It was an era in my life as a football supporter that would probably never be repeated. At the age of eighteen you could say I had already passed my peak in my career as a football supporter.

It was strange then that I did not renew my season ticket and make the most of the last season before I was due to go to university. It had been an unremarkable season just past but even still you would have thought I would have gone to more than four games the following year. I really do not know why I did not go to more.

I was doing a 'gap year' before going to university, working for an insurance company in the City instead of the usual travels abroad people were doing at the same stage in their life. So I definitely had the funds. I suspect my other interests took over. At the start of the season I had been with my first proper girlfriend for six months or so, and was spending a lot of time with her. I was also too influenced by her, and several times I planned to go to the football I did not end up going for some reason or another.

I did have one thing to thank her for, though. She talked me out of going to the Chelsea home game in December. A glutton for punishment, I always tried to go to the Chelsea fixture, but by the end of that afternoon I was thoroughly glad I had not witnessed the embarrassing 6-1 drubbing.

As my first game of that season I went to see a friendly against Fiorentina in early August. Quite apart from the 2-0 loss, I soon realised why I did not like friendlies: there is no particular reason to win and no edge to the proceedings. No meaning and no passion. Being a football supporter is all about winning, and the excitement and hope associated with it. Taking part does not matter at the end of the day. Friendly games do not provide these vital ingredients; they are all about just taking part.

There are only two reasons to go to friendlies that I can see: firstly to see some new summer signings or exciting and skilful opposition players, and secondly to pay tribute to a long serving player in their testimonial year. In this case it was the latter. It was David Howells's testimonial game. At Spurs his entire career, he was a solid midfielder but always underrated and often the forgotten man. It was entirely worthwhile that he should have a day at the Lane devoted to him. Unfortunately, he could not score that day.

The league season started as the last had finished. We recorded very few wins in the first few months and scoring goals was proving very difficult. The result, as so often happens as a knee-jerk reaction in football, was that the manager was sacked.

The Board's decision to let Francis go was understandable given our league position but for some reason best known to themselves they appointed the almost unheard of Christian Gross. In his first press conference the Swiss man bemused all present and watching by waving a tube ticket about, saying how he had come on the London Underground. I was worried; I wanted to know how he was going to improve things at the club, not what his preferred method of transport was.

His appointment turned out to be a disaster and he lasted a year, eventually being sacked for the same reason as his predecessor at about the same stage of the season.

After being put off going to the Chelsea defeat, I finally made it to my first league game of the season just before Christmas. We were playing Barnsley. I could not have timed my return to the Lane any better. We recorded our best result of the season so far, winning 3-0 with goals from Allan Nielsen and two from exciting French winger David Ginola, who we had signed from Newcastle. It was only our fifth league win of the season. Gross was failing to turn things around. That win came in the middle of heavy losses to Chelsea 6-1, Coventry 4-0 and Aston Villa 4-1.

No wonder I was not going more often with results like that. I would have been constantly depressed. Spurs were flirting dangerously with relegation and needed a stronger second half to the season to escape. One solution to help us achieve this delighted me. The club secured the return of Jurgen Klinsmann on a short-term deal for the remainder of the campaign. The hero had returned.

As might have been expected, Jurgen was not able to set the season alight in quite the same way as he had before. As is the case with most films, the sequel proved to be not as good as the first outing. As the campaign approached its final few weeks, Jurgen had failed to pull Spurs to safety. We were still relegation contenders.

With this in mind and quickly realising that I would soon be going off to university, I decided to get a couple of games in before the end of the season. The team needed all the support it could get. The first was a 1-1 draw at home to Everton at the start of April. The second, at the beginning of May, was unforgettable.

There is no doubt what the game of the season was, for the club or for me personally: Wimbledon away. It is always a fun fixture, or at least it was before the club decamped to Milton Keynes. It did not have as intense a rivalry as the other London derbies but the atmosphere at these games was heightened by Spurs fans making up more of the crowd than Wimbledon supporters, including occupying the entire stand at one side of the pitch at Selhurst Park, their rented home. Selhurst Park is not exactly the best ground in terms of facilities for top flight football, but the singing below the low roof at the back of the Arthur Wait Stand would reverberate back towards the fans, increasing the volume of noise created by the supporters.

Spurs needed to win this particular game quite badly as they were in danger of being involved in a last day of the season relegation scrap. A win in this match would ease any fears drastically, and the massed ranks of Spurs away fans were determined to get behind their team and dominate Selhurst Park in terms of noise as well as numbers. It was looking decidedly dodgy at one stage, with Spurs 2-1 down. Luckily, we managed to get it back to 2-2 at half time. Then, almost as though he decided he would turn it on, the returning hero Jurgen Klinsmann decided to give a goalscoring master class in simple finishing, scoring a hatrick in five minutes. He ended up with four in total. A sixth from Moussa Saib meant Spurs were suddenly winning 6-2. We were dancing on the seats, celebrating not only the fact that relegation was no longer possible, but also revelling in Jurgen's wizardry. It was one of those games where hugging strange men was the norm. I fell over at one point. We were singing "it's just like watching Brazil", which was countered sentimentally with "it's just like watching Tottenham". I had seen Spurs score six for the first time, with one of my all-time heroes netting four times. I left the ground buzzing, grinning from ear to ear.

I was certainly in the mood for a party and, luckily enough, I was due to go to one that evening, a friend's house party. I started texting everyone, football fans and friends not interested in football alike: "there's only one Jurgen Klinsmann" and "walking in a Klinsmann wonderland". I received replies, mostly from friends who had no idea I was at a match, let alone who Jurgen Klinsmann was: "why, what's happened?!"

I got the tube over to Ealing and the party got underway early. Rounds of tequila slammers were being drunk in the kitchen and I joined in happily. After a handful of these, everybody got bored with downing shots and got on with the party. Unfortunately for me, I decided I would have a few more and a few more. In fact, I carried on drinking tequila shots until it tasted almost nice, some feat for that particular spirit. That was when it started going a bit hazy; I was stumbling around a little but nothing to get unduly worried about. Then the volume of neat spirits must have hit me and the last thing I remember was being really rather scared as I coughed up blood in the toilet. Five hours later I woke up in Central Middlesex Hospital, with a drip in one arm and a saline feed in the other. Although I have no recollection of those five hours, when I awoke I somehow knew exactly why I was there.

In the meantime, my parents had been called by someone at the party and they duly made the journey to the hospital in the early hours of the morning to visit their unconscious son in a hospital bed. My Dad had been out that night celebrating some rugby win or other and was himself rather worse for wear, and so my Mum drove them to the hospital. When they arrived, I can only but imagine what the hospital staff must have thought of the family, the son in hospital through alcohol abuse and the father turning up to visit him half-cut. The conversation must have gone something like this:

"Hulloo, I'm here to shee Oliver Wright"

"What's he in for?"

"Drinking too mush alcohol [hiccough]."

"And you are?"

"… hish father."

Understandably, although I could not understand it at the time, the hospital staff were very unsympathetic when I came round. They would not phone my parents (who had decided to leave me to it once they knew I was safe) and once they freed me from my medical attachments, I was told to leave, and no they would not show me the way out. I found a payphone to make a call to my parents to ask them to rescue me from the hospital. My Mum answered, repeated my request to my Dad, whose answer was something along the lines of "bollocks!" They had only just got home after their first visit: with my Mum unfamiliar with London roads, and my Dad not with it in the passenger seat, they had ended up going in the wrong direction round the North Circular, ironically nearly reaching Tottenham. In the end I got a friend to pick me up. One thing I did learn from the unfortunate saga was that a drip is a rather good hangover cure, although I would not recommend having to need one.

5. We're the famous Tottenham Hotspur and we're going to Wembley

There was a point, when supporting Tottenham was about the most important thing in my life, when I had decided I was not going to go to university if it meant I could not go and see Spurs every week. My initial solution to this crisis was Middlesex University, who had a campus on White Hart Lane in Tottenham. Perfect. I could be at university and walk to the games in a matter of minutes.

I was about fifteen when I declared this intention. Luckily, by the time university applications were due, I was old enough to re-evaluate my priorities. Instead of insisting on being in or around the capital, I decided that experiencing living somewhere completely different was what I wanted. Sheffield made a good impression on me when I visited and ended up being my destination come September 1998. I spent a total of four years there. Obviously this meant that the opportunities for getting to see my beloved Spurs were going to be limited, not only by the distance but also by the finances.

The prospect of watching Sheffield Wednesday or United to get my football fix did not really appeal, and, in fact, Spurs never once played either club in Sheffield while I was in the city. Both clubs were in the lower divisions for the majority of time I was there, and any matches that did occur did so while I was back in London for the holidays. Living in Sheffield did open up the possibility of getting to some of the northern away games quite easily. It was through this and some home games in the university holiday periods that I managed to attend up to half a dozen games a season during my university career. It was less often than I would have liked but I had a new life in the North, new friends to meet and other things of importance to experience. I went when I could but the start of university would end the possibility of going to see Spurs on a regular basis; I did not know it then but it also marked the start of me only being an occasional match-goer not just while in Sheffield but probably for ever.

Not being able to see Tottenham play as often as I would have liked was offset by the wonderful opportunity of living a university life in Sheffield. I was fortunate enough to meet my future wife and some lifelong friends in my time there. I am also sure that the lifestyle that university provided was the best and most varied I will ever experience: the excitement of living away from home by yourself for the first time; the first real opportunity to establish yourself and your life as you wish; surrounded by a ready-made social circle; everybody open-minded with a general lack of prejudice; a fantastic opportunity to learn (although this probably was not appreciated fully at the time); deciding not to go to a lecture if it was too early; being able to go out every night (I think my all-time record was six nights in a row); no dependants; going to the gym in the afternoon after your lectures had finished for the day; about four to five months holiday a year; the opportunity to travel in the summer holiday; knowing so many people around and about; not worrying about cleaning the house – student houses are meant to be messy; sitting in the union bar's garden all afternoon without feeling guilty; knowing that being silly and acting the fool was acceptable and sometimes expected. I do not envisage being able to have such a fun lifestyle in any other realm of life.

I managed to get to a couple of home games at the start of the 1998/99 season before the university term started. The first, somewhat ironically given my impending new home, was against Sheffield Wednesday. Unfortunately, it was a truly awful performance. Wednesday were 2-0 up when the players were roundly booed off at half time. It got no better in the second half as their left-back, Andy Hinchcliffe, compounded our misery with a curling free kick into the top corner. The whole team looked poor that day; if this was the current standard of football at White Hart Lane, I need not have worried about being 200 miles away. The game finished 3-0 and boos echoed round the stadium once more at the full time whistle.

The last match I saw before I left for Sheffield was at home to Blackburn Rovers. I was hoping for a good send off. It was also about time, I thought, to introduce my girlfriend of the time to the delights of Tottenham Hotspur. She had no interest in football, but seemed relatively keen nonetheless to come with me. After the poor performance against Sheffield Wednesday, I was not exactly showing off the team at the best time. In fact, the atmosphere was a little subdued as well with a fair few empty seats around the ground.

Spurs seemed to carry on from where they had left off last time I had seen them, and within ten minutes were 1-0 down. This time, though, the players rallied and fifteen minutes later we were level through a Les Ferdinand header from a David Ginola cross.

The Spurs players were battling and there was a marked improvement from the Wednesday game, the woeful central defender, Ramon Vega, apart. Five minutes into the second half, their perseverance paid dividends as Allan Nielsen scored with another header from another Ginola cross, a goal that proved to be the winner. The win meant we were eighth in the league, even though the start to the season had been far from convincing. The team had given me a good send off up north too.

I am not really sure what my girlfriend thought of the experience as three weeks later she was my ex-girlfriend. Maybe trying to turn her into a Spurs fan was one step too far?

I spent the next few months settling into university life and did not get to see Spurs again until a mid-term break at the beginning of February. Reading week I think they called it, but I basically used it as a holiday; there was not much reading to do in the first year of a Geography degree.

By this time Christian Gross's reign had finally, and thankfully, come to an end. His appointment was a strange one in the first place and he really had failed to inspire during his year at White Hart Lane. Unfortunately, the new manager turned out to be even worse. The Spurs Board, in their infinite wisdom, decided that George Graham, ex-Arsenal legend (until the bung scandal, of course), was the right man to lead Tottenham Hotspur. Granted, he had put together a very good young team at Leeds since his days at Highbury but his history with Arsenal was too much to bear. The Spurs fans hated him. He achieved success at Arsenal based on a defensive and long-ball game. Arsenal fans were happy singing "1-0 to the Arsenal" all the time, but this was not the way Tottenham fans expected to see their team play. Few gave him a chance. It looked like a disastrous appointment from day one.

To give him some credit, though, he stabilised Tottenham's league position that year; we eventually finished eleventh, higher than we would have under Gross. And, much to my delight, he led the team on two great cup runs.

Indeed, it was an FA Cup fourth round replay against Wimbledon that I saw that February. Spurs stayed on course for Wembley with a 3-0 victory. Many fans stayed away again, however, perhaps due to some disillusionment with Graham's appointment. Nevertheless, it was a convincing performance, striker Les Ferdinand having a particularly good game.

I actually almost missed the start of the match. As I neared Waterloo on the train, I realised I had left my ticket at home. The train to Waterloo took 40 minutes so there was no time to return home and come back again. I would miss the whole first half if I did. So I phoned home. Sensing my distress, my Dad kindly hopped on the next train to meet me at Waterloo with my ticket. It meant that by rushing through London, I made it to my seat just as the game was starting. No sooner had I taken my seat, was I up on my feet again celebrating a goal from Andy Sinton, who had dribbled into the area and unleashed a shot into the top corner. Allan Nielsen added two further goals in the second half, the second scored rather bizarrely as the ball bounced off his knee into the net as he blocked an attempted clearance on the edge of the area, to complete an easy victory.

Having missed out on seeing Spurs at Wembley in 1991 for the semi final and final, and then again seeing them lose to Everton in the semi final four years later, time was running out to fulfil my ambition of seeing Spurs play at Wembley before it was to be rebuilt. I have been to several England matches there, both friendlies and World Cup qualifiers, and even the Sherpa Van Trophy Final between Wolves and Burnley in 1988. I find it hard to get excited about England friendlies, which, with nothing at stake and umpteen substitutions, do not get the fan in me going. I support Spurs over and above the national team, and whilst I like to see England do well and win, I cannot get as passionate about an international game as I inherently am about each and every game Tottenham play. I wanted to see Spurs there, and win there.

To fulfil this ambition entirely, the match would have been an FA Cup final, but Spurs reached the 1999 League Cup final, having beaten Wimbledon over two legs in the semi. I could not have been more excited at the prospect of both watching Spurs in a cup final for the first time and seeing them play under the twin towers. People say there was a lack of atmosphere in that stadium and that you were too far from the pitch, but there was something special about the prospect of witnessing Spurs win a cup final at the most famous stadium in the world.

I found out I had been successful in the postal ballot when my Mum phoned me in Sheffield to say that a ticket had arrived at home. I was overjoyed. This was one of the reasons I remained a member while I was at university: the opportunity to get tickets for big cup games. Well, that and being able to say I was a member of Tottenham Hotspur Football Club.

When matchday finally arrived, I made sure I left plenty of time to get to the stadium so I could soak up the atmosphere before the match. I remember walking out of Wembley Park tube station, and seeing the twin towers emerging in front of me as I walked towards the stadium. There was an excitement in the air at the prospect of Spurs winning a trophy for the first time in eight years. I took my seat high up behind one of the goals. I was nervous waiting for the game to start, but I was trying to take in every detail of the stadium and enjoy everything about the afternoon. Despite my nervousness, I was confident we would win.

The game itself was not a spectacle for the neutral. The only real flashpoint had been our left-back Justin Edinburgh's sending off for lightly stroking Leicester midfielder Robbie Savage's blond flowing locks. Savage made the most of it and the referee produced the red card. It had not been an attractive game to watch and there was little in terms of goalmouth action. Nil-nil and into injury time, the game was heading for extra time and then penalties. Then, in the 93rd minute Steffen Iversen broke down the right and crossed weakly. The Leicester goalkeeper Kasey Keller parried, but only as far as Allan Nielsen who sent a diving header into the back of the net. Ecstasy. I could not believe it and was jumping around for sheer joy. It was so far into injury time that I knew that I had just seen a last minute winner for Spurs, in a cup final, at Wembley. The scenario was perfect.

A few minutes later, Sol Campbell climbed the famous Wembley steps to lift the trophy. There is an air of anticipation as you watch your captain make his way up those steps; it took much longer than when there is a podium in the middle of the pitch. I had seen this many times on television and now I was witnessing it for real. My throat sore, we were singing "when Sol went up to lift the League Cup, we were there, we were there". I was there, waiting for that trophy to be thrust into the air.

Despite the discontent among Spurs fans at George Graham being the manager of their beloved club, no one could argue with the fact that he had led them to their first trophy in eight years. He also led them to an FA Cup semi final three weeks later.

Buoyed by the recent cup final and living in hope that my apparent curse where the FA Cup was concerned might be lifted, I looked forward to an FA Cup semi final against Newcastle at Old Trafford. I had again been successful in the ballot and it was a short trip to make from Sheffield to Manchester. I was so hoping for a win that could finally cast a shadow over that semi final against Everton four years previously.

I thought the omens were looking good when I took my seat. We virtually had three sides of the ground, just as Everton had had at Elland Road. Newcastle fans occupied the massive stand on one side of the ground. What I had not anticipated was the noise they would make. They are renowned for their support and they were probably more desperate for cup success than me; Newcastle last won a trophy in the 1950s.

My seat was behind one of the goals and very close to the Newcastle supporters. The Spurs fans, trying our best to make some noise, were completely drowned out by the sea of black and white next to us. The noise they made throughout was the loudest I have ever heard inside a football stadium. Thankfully, all quietened down for a deafening one minute silence before the match in memory of the Hillsborough disaster ten years previously.

The game was another nail-biter like the League Cup final, although better in quality. The first half had few chances for either side, Spurs trying to play on the break but often resorting to long balls (from a George Graham team, surely not). The turning point came in the 57th minute when the Newcastle centre-back, Nikolas Dabizas, blatantly handled a cross in the Newcastle area. Amazingly, the referee did not award a penalty. As it turned out that was the chance that could have given Spurs a place in the FA Cup final. The half continued with chances for both teams but no goal. Spurs did play well enough to sneak a win after the incorrect handball decision but could not muster a goal.

As extra time started, memories of that horrible Nottingham Forest penalty shoot out sprung to mind. I did not want to go through that again, and neither did either team as both sides had several chances to win it. The Spurs fans were getting behind their team so much. We even sang the taboo lyric "George Graham's blue and white army". Our reluctance to sing the manager's name had up until then resulted in the song "The man in the raincoat's blue and white army", something that was still sung following the League Cup final victory.

I thought one goal would surely win the tie, and I was willing the ball into the net. Then, a moment of horror. Sol Campbell handled in the area and the referee pointed to the spot. Shearer stepped up to take the penalty and slotted the ball home into the goal right in front of me. There were only ten minutes left, and although Armstrong did have a one-on-one with their goalkeeper, I knew deep down I was about to witness another semi final defeat. Sure enough, as if to confirm my fears, Shearer powerfully hit the ball into the top corner from the edge of the area in the last minute to wrap up their victory. I followed the ball all the way into the net as I was right in the line of sight as it travelled through the air. It was galling to watch Shearer wheeling away in delight past me to celebrate in front of the ecstatic Newcastle fans, whose celebrations had turned up the volume of noise coming from them to even higher levels. Gutted, I left the stadium at the final whistle. The fact that I only had a short journey home was scant consolation. My 1995 Everton demons had been far from banished; they were now joined by Newcastle ones.

A week later, I made another short trip to Nottingham Forest. The team managed to shrug off the disappointment of Manchester, and put in a spirited performance. Despite Crossley saving yet another Tottenham penalty, this one from Allan Nielsen, Spurs won 1-0. Iversen got the winner after about an hour, and came to celebrate right in front of where I was sitting in the front row behind the goal. It was a good feeling to be celebrating almost with the players. The result went some way to getting me over the semi final defeat; it was good to have a win to enjoy so quickly.

I spent much of that summer travelling around America, mainly California, Nevada and New York, with my good friend Catherine, both of us taking advantage of the long university holiday. The September start back in Sheffield allowed me to take in a match early in the new season, at home to Everton. This game summed up why you should never leave a game early. Tottenham have an enviable record against Everton, who only in 2006 won at White Hart Lane for the first time since 1985, but we went behind twice and were losing 2-1 with ten minutes remaining.

Both Everton goals were almost identical. On each occasion Ian Walker brought down the Everton striker, Francis Jeffers, and David Unsworth banged home both penalties, the second of which put Spurs 2-1 down with fifteen minutes left. In between these two moments of madness by Walker, Tim Sherwood had headed a goal for Spurs from a corner.

Just as it looked like it would not be our day, Ginola crossed for Oyvind Leonhardsen to rifle home high into the net: 2-2 and game on. Spurs so often seem to score late goals against Everton, and as if scripted we scored a winner four minutes later. The ground erupted in euphoria as Iversen headed home. The late comeback was inspiring and I left the ground on a high.

Tottenham so often in the past seemed to have at least one extraordinary flair player in their team. Since I first started supporting them, I have been lucky enough to see the likes of Hoddle, Waddle, Gascoigne, Lineker, Sheringham, Klinsmann and David Ginola. The current star player is world-class striker Dimitar Berbatov, while nippy winger Aaron Lennon provides a bit of flair down the wings. Ginola joined Spurs in 1997 and was the jewel shining among Graham's otherwise mainly drab team. His skill, ability to beat a man and produce a pinpoint cross or powerful shot were almost second to none at his peak. He was probably the most individually skilful player at White Hart Lane since Paul Gascoigne. He was, in short, a joy to watch. His style was epitomised by a goal against Barnsley in the cup run of the previous season. Picking the ball up on the left flank, he danced inside one player, before advancing past several more as though they were not there on his way into the penalty area and then coolly slotting home under the goalkeeper. A true moment of class, akin to Ricky

Villa's memorable 1981 FA Cup winning goal. Of the two, Ginola's was probably better and had it been scored in as high a profile situation as Villa's, it would have been talked about for decades, too.

Ginola's flamboyant talent did not fit in with Graham's flair-less ethos, however, and by the end of the 1999/2000 season Ginola had been forced out of White Hart Lane.

For one season, the FA decided to abandon tradition and move the FA Cup third round to mid-December. Luckily it was quickly moved back to the first weekend of the new year for the following season. Spurs were drawn at home to Newcastle. This was an opportunity for some faster than anticipated revenge for the semi final defeat eight months previously. This, coupled with the chance to experience the White Hart Lane cup atmosphere, meant I made a special trip down from Sheffield to catch the game. The weekend may also have coincided with a party of some description.

There was the usual array of Wembley and cup songs, the rest of the crowd also sensing a vengeful victory and the start of another cup run. The players responded to this and edged a goalless first 45 minutes. Finally, Spurs took the lead ten minutes into the second half. Ginola crossed wickedly for Iversen to send a diving header into the net. I was jumping for joy with those around me, banishing some of the pain from the semi final. Unfortunately, the goal spurred on Newcastle, rather than us, and they equalised late in the game.

My frustration with Shearer was spilling over. It had, unreasonably, annoyed me when he had run in front of the area of Old Trafford I was in to celebrate getting to the cup final with the Newcastle fans. He also had a knack of winning free kicks by backing into defenders and somehow making it appear as though he was the one being fouled. When his physical tactics did not work, he would complain vocally to the referee. His behaviour was not appreciated by the Spurs fans, myself included.

The game ended all square and a replay, although not the end of the world, was disappointing after taking the lead. The tie was to get infinitely worse, though, as Newcastle won the replay 6-1. There was to be no revenge.

My only other game that season was during the Easter holiday. With nothing really to play for and mid-table mediocrity ensured for yet another season, I made the trip from Cambridge (where I had been out the night before) to see the fixture against Aston Villa.

The journey seemed entirely worthwhile after 47 minutes. Tottenham were 2-0 up through an Iversen header and Chris Armstrong, and the match had been very entertaining. It changed beyond all recognition after an hour. A Spurs outfield player saved a shot on the line with his hands. After initially giving a goal kick, the referee consulted his linesman. After what seemed a confusing eternity, he gave a penalty. Dion Dublin scored to pull one back but nobody could have expected what followed. Twelve minutes later we were 4-2 down after a display of world-class goalscoring. First, Dublin scored again with an overhead volley from the edge of the penalty area into the top corner. Then a minute later the Italian playmaker Carbone scored with a dipping shot, again into the top corner, from outside the area. The amazing comeback was completed when their full-back Alan Wright scored with a first time shot from 25 yards. The Villa fans could hardly have believed their luck; they must have been on cloud nine.

Although I was gutted by the afternoon's happenings, the quality of all the Villa goals, scored directly beneath where I was sat in the Paxton Road upper tier, meant I had little to feel aggrieved about. We had been beaten by a mixture of sublime finishing and freak luck.

George Graham's first (and only as it turned out) full season had ended in two early cup exits and a finish of tenth in the league. We were never threatened by relegation but Spurs were rapidly becoming epitomised by middle table finishes. It was hardly inspiring.

The first match I went to in the following season (2000/01) was in my university reading week in November. I had come home for the week and had bought a ticket for the Sunderland match, which would surely be an easy victory.

In the close season, Graham had bought the exciting Ukrainian forward Sergei Rebrov for what is still a club record £11 million. I am sure he, nor us, the fans, did not appreciate then how he would be destroyed by the managers he served under and what a waste of money he would turn out to be. He eventually left a few years later, his career in tatters, for free.

Although Spurs started the game well, backed by good support from the stands, Sunderland won a penalty after about half an hour following a handball from the hapless Ramon Vega. To my delight Kevin Phillips sent his kick well over the crossbar. Spurs capitalised on this good fortune by taking the lead just before half time, the then captain Tim Sherwood netting following a goalmouth scramble.

As is so typical of Spurs, however, we could not make the game safe and Sunderland equalised half way through the second half. Rather surprisingly and contrary to how they seemed to react in those days, the players responded positively to conceding an equaliser and fifteen minutes later Armstrong scored what turned out to be the winner by nut-megging the goalkeeper when through on goal.

It was hardly a convincing performance against one of the division's poorest teams but at least I had seen a victory.

In the hope of witnessing another win, I chose to take advantage of my northern location and make a short trip to see Spurs play at Bradford on a wet and cold December afternoon. They were newly promoted to the Premiership and dead certs to return to whence they came.

A certain Ledley King had broken through into the first team, and was playing in midfield. There was a good atmosphere in the stand we were in behind the goal, fuelled by an increased sense of togetherness caused by the miserable weather and the fact that most Spurs fans had travelled much further than I had to be there.

The supporters were rewarded far quicker than we may have hoped. Ledley King scored the fastest ever Premiership goal after just ten seconds (a record that still stands as I write). It was a deflected effort that nestled into the bottom corner of the net, and it was his first goal for Tottenham. I was almost too stunned to celebrate. You do not normally expect that from the kick off; the ball normally goes out of play or gets passed around the back four as the players settle.

The early goal set up the match to be a topsy turvy affair. Bradford equalised a few minutes later, but Sol Campbell restored our lead half way through the first half. These first two Spurs goals were at the far end of the ground from us. As Sol ran back to his defensive position in front of us, the whole stand stood to sing his name. It was a nice moment.

Spurs were playing well against a poor Bradford side and extended their lead soon after half time when Armstrong tapped in down in front of us. The game was surely safe now. Had I learned nothing from supporting Spurs? Games are never safe until the final whistle is blown where this club is concerned.

With twenty minutes remaining, Bradford pulled a goal back. It was still no great cause for concern though if we carried on playing like we were. As the rain intensified, however, we defended deeper and deeper until, in the last minute, Bradford claimed their equaliser.

It would have been a hugely disappointing result anyway, but to finish 3-3 after being 3-1 up against the bottom side just was not good enough.

Luckily the people who set the fixture dates had scheduled the north London derby at White Hart Lane for the week before Christmas, which meant I would be back from Sheffield for the season's holiday. It was a Monday night game, live in front of the Sky cameras, and the atmosphere was, as usual, bubbling well before kick off, aided by the giant televisions showing clips of great derby moments from the past.

The game opened in a lively manner, as is the norm in these matches, but developed into a fairly open contest during the first half. The breakthrough we had been waiting for came after half an hour. Darren Anderton's shot from the edge of the box was parried by the Arsenal goalkeeper straight into an onrushing Rebrov, who dived to head home. The goal ensured that despite Rebrov's hardly illustrious Spurs career, he would be remembered fondly in some way in the years to come. He had scored against Arsenal. The Lane went berserk. "1-0 to the Tottenham" was the chorus until half time.

The game changed after the interval and Arsenal dominated proceedings. Neil Sullivan in the Spurs goal made a series of saves to keep us in front. It was nail-biting stuff. Would we hold on? It looked as though Sullivan would produce a heroic display to give us a memorable victory.

The level of hatred between Tottenham and Arsenal was evidenced early in the second half. The ball went out of play into the Spurs crowd for an Arsenal throw-in. As Robert Pires went to retrieve the ball, the fan holding it threw it hard at Pires instead of just handing it to him. This understandably incensed the Frenchman, who, possibly not understanding the intensity of the match, confronted the fan. This, obviously, did not go down too well with the crowd and Pires was the subject of a substantial amount of verbal abuse. The Arsenal midfielder was so riled he soon got himself booked for a bad tackle on Tim Sherwood, and was substituted a few minutes later for Patrick Vieira.

As the match reached is final few seconds, with a win over Arsenal for the first time in a few years looking virtually assured, it was Vieira who rose highest to head home an equaliser in the last minute, just as I had witnessed at Bradford a week earlier. We had very nearly held out despite the pressure and to be denied victory in the closing moments in the derby match, and for the second week running, was devastating.

Tottenham did not have a great team during this period in their history. Players such as Alton Thelwell, Gary Doherty, Stephen Clemence, Willem Korsten and the on-loan Andy Booth were never going to set the Premiership alight. I am not trying to single anybody out for blame; these are just examples in a squad of poor quality. It had been a problem for Spurs for several years. Since the days of

Klinsmann, Sheringham, Barmby and Anderton at his best, Tottenham simply had not had a good enough team. Sol Campbell was the one shining light at that time around the turn of the decade.

It was such a poor team that I saw Spurs lose dismally at Derby County in March 2001. Derby were relegation fodder and very beatable. It should, therefore, not have been the case that Derby dominated the game and were 2-0 up after half an hour. The vocal Spurs end, selling out all their tickets as they nearly always did for away matches, deserved better. The only joy we were afforded was with twenty minutes remaining when we finally scored via an own goal. It was hardly worth celebrating and I never had any confidence we could go on and take something from the game.

The supporters were getting impatient with Graham after yet another poor performance. He had failed to assemble a better team than he had inherited and the fans were watching drab, often long-ball football, something not well tolerated at White Hart Lane. The fans did not need an excuse to call for the dismissal of Graham, who was hardly the popular choice in the first place.

There were increasing clamourings for Glenn Hoddle to be instated as the Spurs boss. He was doing well with Southampton after his England tenure came to a premature end. He had been the King of White Hart Lane and most supporters saw his return as manager at some point as inevitable.

The fans got their way, too. Before the end of the month, Graham was gone and Hoddle, the prodigal son, was the new Tottenham manager. It was what all fans had been waiting for. We truly believed he could bring the glory days back to the Lane.

His first game in charge could not have been much bigger. On 8th April 2001, Spurs played Arsenal again in the FA Cup semi final; it was the third such meeting between the two sides at this stage of the competition in eleven seasons. I was hoping it would also be my third FA Cup semi in seven years. Having been bitterly disappointed by the first two and not having had much, if any, personal FA Cup cheer while supporting a club that is reputed for its cup pedigree, I felt it was going to be third time lucky. I was sure there was some irony in Hoddle's return, too. I had seen his last goal for Spurs in the first game I ever went to against Oxford United in 1987. I then found myself hoping to go to his first as manager fourteen years later.

The week before the match I was in Tunisia on a Geography field trip. I had applied to the postal ballot for a ticket but was not due to find out if I had been successful until that week beforehand. A week of working hard and playing hard culminated in an all night party before we flew back to Manchester and then a big night out the Saturday we got back, which was the day before the match.

To my delight, waiting for me on my return from Tunisia was an FA Cup semi final ticket. I was over the moon. Completely knackered and after very little sleep, I made the short train journey back across to Manchester, where I had landed less than 24 hours previously.

The atmosphere was building in the streets outside the ground as I made my way to the stadium. I took my seat high up in the old Stretford End behind the goal in good time to soak up the pre-match atmosphere. I was so excited and the adrenaline was putting my tiredness to the back of my mind.

We were underdogs. Player for player, Campbell apart, they were better in every position, but I was hopeful, more than that, confident we could sneak a result. I had to see an FA Cup semi final victory at some stage and what better time than now against Arsenal.

Despite my heartfelt confidence, my brain was telling me we would have to be very lucky to get a win. Nevertheless, to my delight and disbelief, we took the lead after thirteen minutes; luck was smiling on us. The ball bobbled around in the box and accidentally found its way to the head of Gary Doherty and into the corner of the net. He did not know much about it but it did not matter. We were 1-0 up in the semi final against Arsenal. My tiredness firmly banished, I was jumping around the stand in ecstasy, just like everyone around me. We could not believe our luck. My heart was not thanking me for this. The hard part would be to hold on to the lead now, which was easier said than done.

Everything changed just after the half hour mark, and I do not just mean the game. Sol fouled Arsenal's long-serving midfielder Ray Parlour and went down in pain himself. He went off the pitch to get treatment. From the resulting free kick Vieira headed home unmarked, just as he had done in the league encounter a few months previously. From that moment I knew we were doomed. To make matters worse our talisman, Campbell, could not return to the action and was replaced by the young Ledley King. As it later turned out, it was Campbell's last game in a Spurs shirt and Ledley would not just replace him in this game, but he would later take his place in the Spurs team and as captain.

Arsenal dominated the whole game, as you would have expected when you looked at the two teams, and it seemed only a matter of time before they found another goal.

Sensing the team needed the help of many more men, the Spurs end responded by turning up the volume in the second half. Maybe we could give the players some added inspiration. The noise was incredible. There were prolonged periods of chanting "Glenn Hoddle's blue and white army", the fans revelling in a manager they could call their own, and my favourite chorus "We are Tottenham, super Tottenham, we are Tottenham from the Lane." Come on you Spurs. Despite the incessant noise, the supporters' efforts were in vain as, try though they might, the players could not get enough of the ball to create any clear cut chances. We were having to defend at all costs.

The singing continued until, with sixteen minutes to go an incisive Arsenal break finished with Pires tapping in. I knew that the match was over; there was no way we could come back. The players sensed it too and the remainder of the match was played out painfully. I just wanted it to end.

I could not have really expected any more. It was a disappointing performance but, and it galls me to say this, we were not able to compete with a superior team on the day. Hoddle had a lot to do for the club to progress, but at least we had the right man in charge at last. He could not have changed things overnight.

As the final whistle blew, it signalled a fourth consecutive FA Cup semi final loss for Spurs and a third for me personally. I was devastated and as the Spurs contingent left the Arsenal fans to celebrate, another wave of tiredness hit me and I admit a solitary tear rolled down my cheek as I descended the stairs to underneath the stand.

It was becoming the one fixture for which I would have done anything to witness a win. The FA Cup is such a special tournament for Spurs fans. We all love the never-ending romanticism and history the club has with the competition. There is always an extra buzz for the matches, a completely separate set of songs, and the atmosphere is aided greatly by the requirement of the home side to offer 15 per cent of seats to the away supporters. There is more excitement as it is a knock out competition; you cannot make up for a loss in the following week's fixture as you can in the league. And there is the ultimate prize of getting to Wembley. The final is the biggest single day in English football and is watched by more people across the world than any other club game. There is so much history associated with final day, so many glory moments. It was also the one competition where the teams climbed the steps into the crowd to collect the trophy, rather than stepping onto a podium on the pitch. And of course, Spurs had a chance every year, unlike in the Premiership.

Of course, in recent years the final has been held at Cardiff's Millennium Stadium. While it was undoubtedly a success at this venue, the competition can only benefit from its return to the new Wembley. Hopefully the new stadium can create its own history to rival that of its predecessor. It is widely recognised that there has been a lull in the FA Cup over the last few years, a period that has coincided with the absence of a final at Wembley to play for. "Spurs are on their way to Cardiff" does not quite sound right.

My season ended on another dismal note as Chelsea came to White Hart Lane and won easily 3-0. There were goals from Hasselbaink, Poyet and Gudjohnsen and a red card for our midfield player Willem Korsten. Playing for more than half the match with ten men, and with central defender Gary Doherty playing as a striker, meant I was relieved the score did not rival Chelsea's 6-1 drubbing at the Lane in 1997. Of course, they constantly remind us of that afternoon by adapting our famous song "we are Tottenham, super Tottenham, from the Lane", to sing "we won 6-1, we won 6-1, we won 6-1 at the Lane".

We were outclassed by a quality Chelsea team and a long injury list meant our team was stretched to its bare bones.

Worse news was to come. Sol Campbell had been immense for Spurs over the past few seasons, a world class player among a very mediocre Premiership team. There had been much speculation he would leave for a team more worthy of his talents, which was entirely understandable given the standard of his fellow team mates. One such rumour stated that Manchester United were interested for £15 million. Nevertheless, Spurs wanted to keep him and the player himself seemed to reject the rumours. The fans were desperate for him to stay. We all knew he was out of contract at the end of the season and time was running out for him to sign a new one. As it turned out, it seemed he had every intention of leaving all along. One of the problems the fans had with that is that he waited until he could leave for free. Instead of Spurs being able to sell him with time remaining on his contract, Campbell's decision meant that it was he who would profit and not the club that had brought him through the ranks, turned him into a Premiership footballer and paid his wages. To make matters worse he did the unthinkable. He joined Arsenal. Having, apparently, at one time said he would not go to our north London neighbours he signed on a massive joining fee and extortionate salary, leaving Spurs empty handed.

As a fan, I can understand players wanting to leave to further their career; Sheringham and now Michael Carrick have done just that and neither is held in the same regard as Campbell. He is vilified every time he returns to the Lane, and the hatred is so strong not just because of what he did, but how he did it. That is why he is referred to as Judas in the stands at White Hart Lane. I, like most Spurs supporters, felt betrayed.

Campbell's replacement at centre-back, and eventually as captain, was Ledley King. Another player to come through the Spurs junior ranks, he was in the Campbell mould: strong and fast, but with the added bonus of being comfortable on the ball and able to pass it well, skills that Campbell lacked. As it was sung, "You can stick Sol Campbell up your arse (repeat a few times) … 'cos we've got Ledley at the back (repeat a few times)". In fact the first time they played on opposing sides, Ledley was the superior performer.

Although Campbell had gone, Hoddle was now at the helm. For this reason alone there was much to be optimistic about for the coming seasons. He would surely restore the attractive passing game that Spurs fans were used to, and ensure his team played in the manner he did as a player. Just maybe he was also the man to make Spurs great again.

6. About time

Hoddle's first full season in charge, the 2001/02 campaign, started very positively. The club looked to be progressing under his leadership and we were once again playing the type of football we were accustomed to. He had brought Sheringham back to the Lane from Manchester United, where he had enjoyed an incredibly successful four years including winning the treble and being named Footballer of the Year. He had achieved what he left Spurs to do. No one really blamed him at the time for leaving Spurs to join the best team in the country. His talent deserved it. His experience, vision and ability would be vital to Spurs even at this late stage in his career.

By the time I got round to seeing my first game of the season as Christmas approached, Hoddle seemed to have worked some of his magic. Spurs were placed seventh in the league table and only six points off the top. We were due to play bottom club Ipswich twice in three weeks, giving us a good opportunity to cement our lofty league position. The first meeting was at White Hart Lane three days before

Christmas. There was an air of expectation around the ground before the game. It was a match we would surely win.

The game began as we expected, too. Within ten minutes, Simon Davies, our young Welsh winger, had put us in front from a Rebrov cross. Regrettably, the game went downhill from there, as Ipswich were allowed to dominate the rest of the half. They got their reward five minutes before half time when they grabbed a deserved equaliser.

Christian Ziege, our left-back, then managed to hit the post and then the crossbar just before and after half time. You might think it sounds as though we were unlucky but had either or both of those efforts gone in, it would have flattered us.

Not long after Ziege's second attempt, Sheringham was incorrectly sent off. His shirt was being pulled all over the place as he waited for a corner. In an attempt to free himself, he swung his arm back and caught the defender's shoulder. The referee deemed this a punch and produced the red card. I could not believe this. A match that had promised so much was going from bad to worse.

Nevertheless, as so often happens, our remaining ten men were spurred on by this incident and constantly attacked the Ipswich goal. We had chance after chance but could not find the net. It looked like we would have to settle for the draw, when with two minutes to go, Ipswich's Alun Armstrong was left unmarked to head home. I seemed to be seeing Spurs concede lots of vital goals in the dying moments at that time.

It was a truly awful evening, and a bad way to start the Christmas period. We had let a team that had not won since August beat us at home.

Our league season really deteriorated from this game and any hopes of European qualification quickly faded. Luckily our League Cup run was still in full swing and a two-legged semi final with Chelsea awaited in the new year. I just had to get to the second leg at White Hart Lane.

Tottenham v Chelsea. 23rd January 2002. League Cup semi final (second leg). Tottenham were never going to win this match. We had not beaten Chelsea for 12 years, a period that extended to 15 years for the last time we beat them at White Hart Lane. Chelsea had comfortably beaten West Ham 5-1 in their previous game, a match I saw at Stamford Bridge, courtesy of my Chelsea-supporting friend Rosie who had a spare seat for the game. My report to Glenn Hoddle would have been something along the lines of "you had better start praying!" Conversely, Tottenham had unconvincingly drawn 1-1 at home to Everton four days previously, somehow amassing 18 corners and not scoring from any of them. And of course we were already 2-1 down before kick off, that being the score in the first leg. Add to this the facts that we had lost the three previous semi finals that I had attended, and the last four matches. These were superstitious facts that started to make my friends wonder why they had paid £28 to come and see the game as they sipped nervously on their beer. We had no chance.

I was seriously contemplating my sanity an hour before kick off. I had driven down from Sheffield, a drive which inexplicably took four hours, due to a single car strangely parked in the outside lane of the M1. Why was I even bothering? We were going to lose anyway, and even if we won, we could still lose overall. I was convincing myself that it was going to penalties. A 2-1 score after extra time would result in this. Unfortunately, it was the night before my girlfriend Sarah's first exam in her final year. This meant that I was not going to be there in the morning to help settle any nerves she would undoubtedly have. All so I could go and watch Tottenham lose, even though I was being my usual eternally optimistic self, saying that we had to win sometime and 2-1 was a likely score to take us to penalties. This was the best scenario in my head. Even the most optimistic person in the world would not have dreamt up the actual score.

I arrived eventually, gasping for a pint, which I consumed in about three minutes at the supporters club due to my extreme thirst and probably stress at endless red and white lines of car lights. There were four of us at the match. The same four who used to have season tickets when we were at school: me, James, Stuart and the unfortunately named Windy, but it just matched his surname so well. (By that time he had unsurprisingly chosen that his preferred name was Andy.) I had been going to see Spurs by myself over the last few years but I had got us all tickets after finding out that they all wanted to go as well. So it was the old team reunited again.

We got into the ground ten minutes before kick off, after selecting the least dodgy-looking dodgy burger stall to buy dinner from. Delicately served by the compulsory overweight man with dirty hands. The atmosphere was electric. Obviously, 33,000 other Tottenham supporters had convinced themselves that this time we would beat Chelsea, and what better time to do it than in a semi final from 2-1 down. We were positioned in the East Stand lower tier, about in line with the penalty spot, seven rows from the front. It was almost directly opposite where I had sat fourteen and a half years ago, which was the last time we had beaten Chelsea at home. As an eight year old, I saw my hero Chris Waddle set up the winner for Nico Claesen five minutes from time in a 1-0 victory. I would have settled for the same score this time around, as it would have meant that we would progress to the final on the away goals rule.

In fact we went 1-0 up after 105 seconds. The ground absolutely erupted. We were jumping around, acting mostly in disbelief. I sustained a bruise on my left calf as a result of jumping a little too vigorously into one of the blue plastic chairs. This meant that my heart would be beating dangerously fast for the remaining 118 minutes (assuming extra time would happen). There will probably be a time when the only games I will be able to go and watch will be the likes of Leicester and Derby at home, purely for health reasons. We had to last until the end of extra time before away goals counted. James said to me that he would only settle when it was 5-0; not very likely was my reply. They would score, at least once, in the huge amount of time left. For the next half an hour though Chelsea did not get into the game and we continued to dominate. What I did not expect was for this to last for the whole game. We scored again on about the thirty minute mark. A trademark low corner was swung in towards the near post and Sherwood hit the top corner with an arrow of a shot. 2-0 at half time and we were dreaming. Chelsea had not been in the game and had not had a shot on target. Their multi-national multi-talented team would surely come out for the second half and take over.

As soon as the second half was underway, it was clear that Spurs were once again dominating. Ten minutes after the break Sheringham scored a screamer. Tottenham were now attacking the goal we were

162

sitting near. I followed his sweetly struck volley all the way into the net. As it bulged, White Hart Lane exploded. We were 3-0 up against Chelsea. This meant that they had to score twice to take it to extra time, still entirely possible with their strike force of Gudjohnsen and Jimmy Floyd Hasselbaink, who had been on fire recently. The latter had scored seven goals in his last four games against us, including the two in the first leg. Neither had had a sniff of goal yet and were being dominated by our young centre-backs King and Gardner. Surely, one would be able to produce something. Most people's fear was that they could still turn it round. Then came the incident that had Chelsea fans whinging. Following a melee in the Spurs penalty area, the referee produced a red card. All we could make out from where we were sitting was that it was a Chelsea player. It took about two minutes for someone to walk off the pitch after the arguments aimed at the referee had calmed down. That player was Hasselbaink, and his walk was accompanied all the way with the fans waving from all directions. In actual fact it was a case of mistaken identity. Their left-back Melchiot was the offender, shoving Teddy in the face. It was irrelevant anyway. We were 3-0 up and Chelsea had not had a shot on goal yet. I was slowly beginning to believe that we would win.

Our domination reached epic proportions after the sending off. Simon Davies was given an unbelievable amount of room and time again down the right flank, just in front of where we were sitting. With a quarter of an hour to go, he received the ball in space, drove infield and struck a shot against the inside of the post, and into the net. Yesssssssssss!!! It was the most celebrated fourth goal I have seen. Normally, by the time you reach 4-0, a gentle cheer and clap is sufficient to greet the goal. This was no normal match though. The

163

fourth goal signalled that we would undoubtedly win; they would need three now to take it into extra time. And this was against Chelsea; we would celebrate every goal with equal energy until it reached 10 probably. We had been annoyingly starved for that long. I already had a sore throat from cheering the first three goals, but I still tested my vocal chords to their full limit for this special strike. It was right in front of us, and the players came and celebrated literally yards from our half-used seats.

This is when it dawned on me that it meant as much to the players that we won as it did to the fans. Any player wants to reach a cup final, but the Spurs players wanted to beat Chelsea, and badly, for the fans as well as themselves. This was confirmed by the substitution of midfielder Gus Poyet. A Chelsea player until the start of that season, he was always loved by the Chelsea fans. Since he had been playing for Spurs, the fans had warmed to him in the same way. As he was leaving the field, he jumped high off the ground, punching the air with delight. The happiness of Glenn Hoddle was also there for all to see. The manager who we had wanted ever since he had started managing was seen jumping out of his seat at the goals, just like the rest of us, on the big screen replays. While he was Chelsea manager, I wonder if it crossed his mind that he would not really have minded if Tottenham had beaten his Chelsea side. *His* side, as he was reminded by the Spurs fans every time Chelsea met Tottenham, was the lilywhites: "You're Spurs and you know you are".

The fifth was scored with five minutes left, and James and the rest of us had the unbelievable cushion of five goals. Chelsea got a consolation that was not even that in the last minute. Rosie, my Chelsea-supporting ex-house mate, missed this finale. She had left her seat in the Chelsea section after the fourth. The last words I had said to her were "we'll beat ya." I had said this not really believing it, but I had been saying "we will beat you next time" for so long now it had just a become a habit. I had only kept saying it so that when it did happen, I could say "told you we'd beat ya," which I did via text message, along with other such things as "can we play you every week."

As the final whistle went, the familiar sound of Chas and Dave singing Glory, Glory Tottenham Hotspur was accompanied by the hoarse voices from all four sides of the ground; well maybe not the West Stand, who managed to stay seated for the majority of the game (the goals apart) while everyone else was on their feet. The West Stand tenants pay more than anyone else in the ground but the majority do not enjoy the game so vocally. Little sound is heard from them. While the rest of the stadium celebrates more vigorously, the West Stand usually sits down again before the rest of the ground has noticed that they have actually stood up. There is nothing wrong such behaviour, clearly, but I need to get personally involved in the match, both animated and vocally active, to enjoy it fully; it is part and parcel of my match experience. I do not mean any of this in a derogatory way; I just do not understand how people stay so outwardly calm and unaffected. Each to their own though.

The six and a half hour, 300 mile round trip had been worth it. The drive home was going to take half as long, and seem infinitely better than the disheartening drive down. We all agreed that evening that it was the best match any of us had been to. Obviously it was more enjoyable than any of the semi finals I had been to; I had now seen us actually win one. It was even better than the 1999 League Cup final, well maybe on a par. The emphatic way in which we won, a semi final, against Chelsea, at the Lane, on a night with an electric atmosphere are the reasons why. The wonderful thing about this match was that it was wonderful from start to finish. Spurs scored goals ranging from the second minute up to three minutes from time, outplaying Chelsea for this entire period. One of my Dad's friends had emailed him in the week previously to say how they were going to stuff us. I emailed my Dad the next day to tell him that it was purely us who did the stuffing.

The beauty of football matches is that in amongst some dreadful performances, you get a diamond of a match like this; one you will remember and treasure for as long as your mind functions.

I think Chelsea detested losing to us like that, probably about the same amount as we loved beating them. They firmly put us in our place by beating us 4-0 twice in four days in March, once in the league and once in the quarter final of the FA Cup. Here's to the next twelve years then.

We were for once unsuccessful in the ballot for final tickets. It may have been for the best as our league form transferred to the final and we lost 2-1 to Blackburn. It was a frustratingly poor performance. I watched the game with Stu in my Union bar in Sheffield.

I only managed to see one other game that season. My final year in Sheffield was a very hectic one and I struggled to find time to get to games. I was determined, however, to make use of being so close to many northern clubs before I returned south for good in the summer. So, I got myself a ticket for the game at Bolton Wanderers in April. By this time we were out of both cups, and were assured yet another mid-table finish. A season that had promised so much had ended quite tamely.

I had never been to the Reebok Stadium before so it was good to add another ground to the list, which as I write contains some 27 different stadia.

The match summed up the second half of Tottenham's season. After an early goal from Iversen, we never really looked like scoring again, and conceded an equaliser due to a defensive mistake. Again, we had failed to beat one of the division's poorest teams.

The game was fairly uninteresting. It was also apparent that our strikers were deteriorating. Sheringham, understandably, was slowing and seemed less capable of influencing a game than he used to be. Meanwhile, Rebrov was completely failing to live up to his £11 million price tag. In the end we were lucky to escape with a draw as Bolton hit the bar, had a goal disallowed and twice had efforts cleared off the line by a defender, all in the closing minutes.

After this match, the inexplicable happened. I did not see my beloved Tottenham Hotspur for about eighteen months, including, obviously, the whole of the 2002/03 season. I still do not know how and why this happened. Despite the lacklustre Bolton game, I do not remember thinking I did not want to go for a while. I know Spurs were constantly finishing mid-table, but there was nothing new there. And anyway, I had only recently witnessed one of my favourite ever games, against Chelsea. I had finished university also and moved back to London, albeit only for a few months until I moved fifty miles further south to Winchester. In any case, I was much closer to Tottenham once more and, as I was earning, I had more money available for tickets. The returning hero, Hoddle, was still in charge, too. I still followed the club closely, watching on television where I could, reading the match reports and being affected by the results. I certainly did not lose any passion for the club during this time, and it definitely was not a conscious decision not to go.

Looking back, the only possible explanation I can think of is that through this season, I was concentrating on getting a career started and at the same time planning my wedding. I still had a full social life, though, and plenty of time to get to some games. It just does not make sense to me.

As it turned out, one point of view might be that it was not such a bad thing. Hoddle's policy had been to assemble an experienced but consequently immobile midfield, including the likes of Sherwood, Poyet and Anderton. We ended my missed league season as we had finished the last, in mid-table, tenth this time. Furthermore, we had exited both cup competitions in the third round. There had been really very little to get excited about. Despite this, I still cannot believe now, though, that I did not go to a single game. It was the first and only season since I began supporting Spurs that I had not been to even one game. It is actually something that I regret and I do not plan to ever make such an omission from my life again.

My season-long absence meant I was chomping at the bit to get back to White Hart Lane when the 2003/04 season got underway. James and Stuart were also keen to get to some games again; since about 1997, I had pretty much been alone in my match-going support. It was good to have some Spurs companions again. We got tickets for the Everton game at the start of October. I was still a member (and had been even in the previous season), while the others were not, which meant we had to buy non-members tickets to be able to sit together.

The day before the match was like being a young boy waiting to go to his first match again, except this time I knew what to expect. I was really quite excited; I kept thinking about the stadium, the fans, the noise of players kicking the ball, the sight that greets you when you step from beneath the stand. I awoke early on match day like an excited child on Christmas morning. It was ridiculous really. I was 24 years old, acting like someone less than half my age. It showed me how much I had missed Spurs. I had a renewed interest and vigour in my support for the club from that day onwards.

Glenn Hoddle had already been sacked by the time of this game in October, amid a very poor start to the season and stories of dressing room unrest. The return of the King had not quite worked out as everyone had hoped. Director of football, David Pleat, was temporarily put in charge until the right replacement had been recruited.

I savoured every moment of the game, from walking up to the stadium from the station to taking my seat and everything about the match. I felt at home again. We were Everton's bogey side too, especially at the Lane, so I was confident of a victory to mark my return. The team started well, passing accurately and creating chances, but it remained goalless as half time approached. Then, two minutes before the break came a moment that made me realise why I have this sometimes painful pursuit. The Spurs goalkeeper, Kasey Keller, kicked long to the head of striker Freddie Kanoute, who touched the ball back to Gus Poyet. The ball, still bouncing, was returned to Kanoute, who sent a first-time dipping shot into the top corner of the goal we were sat behind. The Park Lane stand erupted to greet the magnificence of the goal. It is one of the best I have ever seen live.

To cap off a fine day, Poyet and then Robbie Keane (who had been signed to partner Sheringham the previous season) made it 3-0 in the first four minutes of the second half. In fact, all three goals were scored in just seven minutes of play.

A certain Wayne Rooney came off the bench in the second half, aged only seventeen. He had no effect on the game, other than to run around as though in a bad temper, committing several fouls, complaining to the referee and eventually getting himself booked.

My first match back had gone better than expected: a convincing victory and a wonder goal. I whole-heartedly applauded the team from the pitch as "Glory, Glory Tottenham Hotspur" rang out around the stadium.

In December, I got a ticket at the last minute to see Spurs play Wolverhampton Wanderers at home. The lateness of my decision meant I was able to use my membership but I would have to return to going alone, which was not something I minded too much having got used to it over the years.

Robbie Keane was playing against the team who first brought him to prominence as a teenager. He reminded them what they had first seen in him in style, scoring a well taken hatrick. Despite this, he showed his apparent integrity and respect for the opposing Wolves fans by abandoning his usual cartwheel celebration and instead just calmly trotted back to the halfway line after each of his three goals. They were greeted rather more enthusiastically in the stands! "We all dream of a team of Robbie Keanes", sung to the tune of Yellow Submarine, was the chorus of the day.

The match was an exciting one, even if Spurs were not especially good. Despite this we ran out 5-2 winners.

I was sat back in the Paxton Road end for this game. This was the stand that had been our home back in the mid-1990s when we used to go to nearly every home game. It was the Members' stand back then and tended to have the best atmosphere. In recent years, however, it has been designated the family stand and, in the main, the core atmosphere-generating supporters are now based in the Park Lane stand at the opposite end of the ground. In fact, as of the 2007/08 season, the club has introduced a new scheme to prioritise supporters accompanied by a junior member in the Paxton Road stand. We had watched the Everton game from this new vantage point and the Park Lane end is now our usual area of the ground to sit in, as long as we can get tickets there. It seems to be the noisiest and most party-like area of the ground. It is also next to the away fans, which lends itself to a more intense atmosphere.

The Wolves game was much closer than the scoreline suggests. It was 1-1 at half time and 2-1 with fifteen minutes remaining. Our final three goals, and one more for Wolves, were scored as the evening grew dark and the floodlights lit up the pitch. The game was wrapped up by a superb goal from midfielder Stephane Dalmat in the last minute. He cut in from the right and unleashed a drive that was as straight as an arrow into the top corner of the goal I was behind. Kanoute was Tottenham's other scorer; in fact he also almost managed to repeat his goal against Everton but the Wolves goalkeeper was able to tip the ball over the crossbar.

I was truly enjoying my visits to White Hart Lane again and had seen eight Spurs goals in two matches so far that season. Tottenham's goalscoring, and conceding, was to reach new levels, though, around the time of my next match.

We had chosen to go to the Portsmouth game at the start of February. In the week beforehand, I settled down in a local pub to watch our FA Cup fourth round replay at home to Manchester City. I sat there smugly as we went 3-0 ahead by half time, and through to the next round for sure. The second half brought the unimaginable. City clawed their way back, scoring once, twice, three times and then in the last minute claimed their winner. I was dumbstruck, my face showing my utter disbelief as I sat staring at the television, the only person in the south coast pub who cared either way.

It was a freak match that might happen once a season at most. Not that season though. The next three games were almost identical in drama and goals, although luckily not in outcome.

Three times we went ahead against Portsmouth; each time they equalised. It was probably only through the timing of our fourth goal in the 89th minute that meant it turned out to be the winner. They just did not have enough time to equalise again. If it had been scored a few minutes earlier, I am sure Portsmouth would have pulled level for the fourth time.

Our first goal came from new striker Jermain Defoe, who had joined from West Ham for £7 million in the January transfer window. On the edge of the area, he shifted the ball half a yard to his right and quickly put a low shot inside the post into the bottom corner. It was a sign of things to come for Defoe. Following Pompey's first equaliser, Keane twice put Spurs ahead, each time duly followed by a Portsmouth goal. It was finally made 3-3 with five minutes to go.

With all the goals flying in and the memory of the Manchester City game too fresh in the mind, the Portsmouth fans were singing "we're gonna win 4-3". Some Spurs fans clearly feared the worst, too. They started leaving the ground, getting out before witnessing their second 4-3 defeat in four days.

This time, though, it was Spurs who got the last minute winner, a Gus Poyet header from a corner. We were ecstatic, the vacant seats around us giving James, Stu and I more room to jump around. What a relief. We responded to the Portsmouth fans' earlier song with the same, but now accurate, lyrics: "we're gonna win 4-3".

Amazingly Spurs then managed to win 4-2 at Charlton after being 3-0 ahead and then in their next game drew 4-4 in a calamitous match with Leicester. I listened to the first on the radio and watched the second on television. Neither was good for my nerves.

My final game that season was Arsenal's championship decider at White Hart Lane. I was by myself again, as James and Stu could not get tickets without memberships. I had a seat only a few metres from the Arsenal fans, who were in party mood, sure they would win the Premiership that day.

Spurs had added incentive for this match, not that any is needed for this fixture. If we won, Arsenal would have to wait to seal the Premiership trophy. No Spurs fan wanted to see our arch rivals win the League on our home soil.

Unfortunately, Arsenal started the match as if in no mood to postpone their fate. They dominated the first half completely. I feared the worst after five minutes when Vieira finished off an incisive move that started from a Spurs corner. Pires scored another goal with similar ease. Such was Arsenal's superiority that at half time I feared a scoreline of 4-0 or 5-0 was the most likely outcome. We had not looked threatening in the slightest.

The half time break, however, changed the pattern of the game. The Tottenham team suddenly had the passion and determination that had been lacking in the first half.

Just after the hour mark, our pressure paid off as Redknapp hit a fierce drive into the bottom corner. Buoyed by this, the volume inside the Lane, and especially at the back of the Park Lane lower tier, increased dramatically. We were willing the team to score a second.

Although Arsenal should have extended their lead, Spurs were determined to complete the fightback. Kanoute was given a golden opportunity to do just that. Arsenal had a throw-in deep inside their own half. Their defender was, I think, trying to throw the ball back to the goalkeeper, but he had not spotted Kanoute lingering in the box. The ball fell to his feet. All he had to do was turn and he would have just had Lehmann to beat. The crowd were eagerly urging him on, but Kanoute hesitated, thinking that he could not have been given such an easy chance, and seemingly awaited the referee's whistle. He did eventually shoot but with no conviction; it was a wasted opportunity.

Tottenham's persistence finally paid off in the last minute. As Keane waited on the goal line for a Spurs corner at the Paxton Road end, the Arsenal goalkeeper, Jens Lehmann, seemed to push him over, although I could not really see clearly from my vantage point. After talking to his linesman, the referee booked both players. He then, to my delight, pointed to the penalty spot. Robbie duly dispatched the kick and the noise inside White Hart Lane was deafening as the Tottenham fans celebrated coming from behind to snatch a battling draw against Arsenal.

Unfortunately, it was not enough to prevent Arsenal winning the Premiership that day. It was odd for both sets of fans to celebrate at the final whistle. I had never seen that before. We were happy at our comeback, but Arsenal had the ultimate reason to celebrate: they had just won the League. That realisation quickly dampened any celebrations outside of the red and white north west corner of the ground.

I left along with most Spurs fans to leave the Arsenal party to continue for longer than our momentary cheers. Fortunately, Sol Campbell left the pitch rather than celebrate with his team mates; it was a wise decision in many respects.

Despite seeing so many goals in my four games that season, including seven from Robbie Keane, it had been a far from convincing campaign. We finally finished fourteenth, our worst position for ten years. Not great for my first season back.

That summer I got married to Sarah, who I had met at Sheffield while at university. She was perfect in every way, apart from one thing. She was an Arsenal supporter. Not only that, but I was marrying into a whole family of Arsenal supporters. The one characteristic I would have previously said was a requisite in any future wife was that she did not support Arsenal (or Chelsea for that matter). I somehow managed to overlook it, although it does make some match days rather difficult. Sarah's father, Geoff, of course made the joke, in his father of the bride speech, that our first son would be called Ian. Absolutely no chance.

I do, however, fear that my battle to get any children we may have to support Spurs may be made all the more difficult by this influence from the red half of north London. Trying to stop them supporting Manchester United or Chelsea will be hard enough. I think my tactic should be to try to embed the club in their subconscious from an early age, repeatedly showing them the plethora of Spurs videos and DVDs I have while they are babies, dressing them in the baby clothes the club sells in their shops, and ensuring their soft toys are cockerels rather than bears. They may then associate a cockerel with being happy and comforted as they grow up. I only say all this half in jest. It is a fight I am determined to win, if only to even up numbers a little at family gatherings.

When Glenn Hoddle was sacked towards the start of the 2003/04 season, the club chairman, Daniel Levy, said Tottenham would wait as long as necessary to employ the right long-term manager for the club. There were several mutterings throughout the season about who this would be and some of Europe's highest profile managers were mentioned. While the deliberations continued, David Pleat remained in charge for the rest of the season. Eventually, in the close season the club announced that Jacques Santini, the then France coach, would be the new manager of Tottenham Hotspur Football Club once Euro 2004 had finished. Few supporters believed Santini was the first choice the club had waited the best part of a year for. Luckily, Martin Jol was appointed as his assistant.

The fans hoped for great things after the protracted wait. They did not materialise. Santini turned out to be a defensively-minded coach and we were hardly scoring any goals. Neither were we getting the hoped-for results.

Santini's shortcomings were confirmed the first time we got to see his team in action. About a month into the 2004/05 season we went to see Manchester United at White Hart Lane (James and Stu with their memberships renewed). United were impressive and dominated proceedings. The final scoreline of 1-0 flattered Tottenham. Van Nistolrooy was the scorer, via a penalty. He later also had a goal disallowed. Spurs just could not cope with United's attacking verve. Our new manager was just not producing the goods.

Just three months into the season, Santini proved he was not the man Spurs had been waiting for. He resigned and returned to France, citing personal reasons. Martin Jol took the reigns, initially temporarily, and then permanently. The fans warmed to him immediately and he did not look back.

7. Another new dawn?

Jol continued the rebuilding that he had been a part of when Santini took over. In his first couple of years at the club, enough players were bought to field two or three new teams. The amount the squad changed in such a short space of time, coupled with some evident improvement in the fortunes of the club, shows how much work needed to be done. The older squad members were released and the club's recruitment policy was to buy players who were young, full of potential and, if possible, English. The change was refreshing and brought great optimism to the club, as Jol built for the future.

Martin Jol arrived in English football as a relatively unknown man. He was manager of a lesser first division club in his native Holland and he had apparently once had talks with Sir Alex Ferguson about being the United boss' right hand man. After his appointment as manager at White Hart Lane, he quickly built up a rapport with the fans and established a relationship as one of the nicest managers around. His enthusiasm is clear to see during matches; he delights in every goal and scowls meaningfully on the touchline when things are not going so well. He is a big man, tall and wide, but he has an outwardly gentle personality. Unlike many of his Premiership counterparts, he rarely complains, moans or blames referees for his own team's failings. The prime example of this was in a game at Old Trafford in his first few months in charge. As the game approached the 90 minute mark, the ball fell to one of our midfielders, Pedro Mendes, just inside the United half. He hit it first time hopefully towards goal; their goalkeeper spilled it and it bounced clearly over the line by some two feet. I could see this watching at full speed on my portable 14 inch television at home. Somehow, though, the linesman failed to see it and did not award the goal. The replays and pictures afterwards confirmed what everyone except the match officials knew.

Jol had every right to be disgruntled; his team had been denied a rare victory against Manchester United by an inept linesman. Instead, when asked about the incident in a post-match interview, he merely showed his disappointment and brushed the question aside. He has since admitted, during a rather comical press conference, that he spoke to the linesman personally after the match, and told him in no uncertain terms what he thought of him. But, importantly, he kept his dignity in public, in stark contrast to many other current top managers.

Jol's first match in charge could hardly have been any bigger. It was against Arsenal at White Hart Lane. A midday kick off in N17 is not the easiest to get to if you live in south Hampshire. What makes it especially difficult is running a bit late, the card machines in the station car park not working, a huge queue for the station ticket office and you not being quite as fit as you thought you were. It turned out the particularly early kick off (imposed by the police after the trouble at the fixture the previous year that kicked off at 4.00pm) was also a problem for many hundreds of other fans. The streets surrounding all four sides of the ground were heaving at 11.55 and we missed the start by about two minutes. Obviously a delayed kick off was not considered.

I would have settled for only missing a couple of minutes of the game after missing my train from Winchester. It sparked a mad panic in my head – I had to get to the ground on time. I generally like to be in the ground at least 15 minutes before the start to absorb some of the atmosphere, and, more practically, I had all three tickets, the other two of which were for James and Stu waiting patiently at Waterloo. A mixture of trying to chase the trains up the M3 and sprinting around train and tube stations meant that we nearly got there on time. Given the final score of the game, it is a little surprising that we did not miss any goals!

North London derbies have so much about them to set them aside from other games. They always have the same meaning and importance no matter at what stage of the season they take place or whether one team or both is in a meaningless league position. There is always an atmosphere at these games that, as well as not being matched in volume at nearly all other fixtures, is entirely different to the atmosphere at all other matches. The only problem, most likely borne out of this increased rivalry, expectation and energy, is that north London derbies often lack goals. James pointed this out to me after a goalless first half-hour, where although we were more than matching Arsenal, there was very little goalmouth action. I agreed, but pointed out that there was a 2-2 draw in the same fixture last season.

We went ahead on 37 minutes, a Carrick free kick being missed totally by the Arsenal defence as it was whipped over and carrying through to Naybet at the far post, who duly finished into the bottom corner. Cue mad scenes on all sides of the ground. Unbelievably, for the rest of the match there was a goal, on average, every six minutes! Sloppy defending allowed Arsenal to go in at half time at 1-1. Very disappointing after being ahead in injury time but a draw would not be a bad result. Spurs had played well, passing the ball around and closing Arsenal down to the extent that all their attacking flair players were kept very quiet.

In the first 15 minutes of the second half we witnessed some comical defending, previously more usually associated with mid-nineties centre-back Kevin Scott and more recently Gary Doherty. This was a bit of a shock given our defensively solid start to the season. Anyway, these defensive shockers meant Arsenal went 3-1 up. Even the most optimistic fan must have thought there was no way back now. Just as we were thinking the worst of how the rest of the match might turn out, Defoe turned his defender 35 yards out, ran unchallenged into the box and shot superbly into the top corner. Game back on. Now suddenly every pessimistic fan thought we could get something out of the game. The volume was turned up and the north London derby atmosphere was back at full intensity.

More awful defending gave Arsenal another two-goal cushion, only for Ledley King to bring it back to 4-3. Each time Arsenal put the game beyond doubt we got back into it almost straight away. The same happened again: the ball was given away in defence and Robinson was beaten at his near post, only for Kanoute to bring it back to 5-4 with five minutes left. We could get an equaliser here – fans in all stands were on their feet urging the team forward for some last gasp attacks. In injury time the ball dropped to Simon Davies 25 yards out – had it gone in the roof would have come off the Lane.

Another new era (albeit only four months after the last one) brought, in some ways, the most amazing match I had ever been to. A last minute equaliser would have definitely made it so. Martin Jol had promised attacking football 'the Tottenham way', something all Spurs fans want to hear. The goals and entertainment, along with never giving up, meant that all the players were applauded off; for me there was not the same disappointment as when losing to Arsenal in the past. Maybe it was shock. The game and result could not quite sink in as we walked down from the top of the upper tier of the Paxton Road stand to reveal the big screen confirming the final score of the highest scoring north London derby ever: Spurs 4 Arsenal 5.

Despite an upturn in the team's fortune, for us personally the season was shaping up as a miserable one. Two more defeats, first at home to Chelsea and then away at Southampton, meant that we had only seen Spurs lose all season.

The Chelsea game was frustrating. Although we matched them for periods, you always got the impression they would win. Their play was clinical with an evident lack of flair, akin in style to the top Italian teams. It remained 0-0 until a minute before half time when a blatant Chelsea dive was rewarded with a penalty, which was duly dispatched. Lampard added his and Chelsea's second in the final minute of the game to complete a 2-0 victory. As I left the ground after the final whistle, I thought to myself that I would rather an Arsenal team that played attractive football win the League than a Chelsea side that played this unexciting brand of football.

We were absolutely dreadful in the 1-0 defeat at Southampton. There was very little to cheer sat behind the goal in the new St Mary's stadium. The main reason we went to the game was that it was very close to where I lived and it was also very easy for James and Stu to get to from the edge of south west London. In a way, I wish I had not bothered. Quite apart from the result, the afternoon was not really enjoyable on any front. The atmosphere inside St Mary's was awful. It was not noisy by any means in the Spurs section, all of us uninspired by the performance, but you could hear a pin drop in the rest of the stadium. There was no noise from the Southampton supporters until their goal went in after about an hour. Although The Dell was an appalling stadium aesthetically and from a facilities point of view, at least it had some character and atmosphere.

Through some friends of Stu's with season tickets, we were lucky enough to get tickets for the Liverpool away game in April. Anfield has a certain aura surrounding it that makes matchdays there, I think, the most special away trip in English football. It is a mixture of the tradition and history, both good and bad, a friendly atmosphere and, when they are playing well, the exciting, driving nature of Liverpool's game. Also, Tottenham have only won five league games there ever, the last in 1993. The rarity of these victories also included a 73-year barren run, eventually ended by Garth Crooks in 1985. The hope of witnessing such a rare football event also adds to the anticipation and atmosphere of the day.

The match that season had the added emotion of it being the weekend of the Hillsborough Tragedy anniversary, and the added passion of Liverpool having won through to the Champions League semi final in the week beforehand. It must be one of the most awesome sights in football to be facing the Kop as the teams enter the pitch to "You'll Never Walk Alone". It is *the* football anthem, and to witness it in this charged atmosphere was awesome. There is so much history associated with it and there is something special when the tune strikes up: "When you walk through a storm, Hold your head up high, And don't be afraid of the dark…"

Home fans on all sides of the stadium are covered by scarves and flags, and an echoing and rousing full rendition of this classic football song rings round the stadium. The Kop is especially alive with colour and sound, and is mesmerising to watch. These sights and sounds make the little hairs on the back of your neck stand up and the match has not even started yet. I find Glory, Glory Tottenham Hotspur builds the atmosphere and gets you in the mood for the game, but it is well beaten by this pre-match five minutes at Anfield.

It is a sad thought that a few years after this match, Anfield would be no longer. As I had just seen an example of at Southampton, over the previous decade, many clubs had abandoned their traditional homes to move to new purpose built all-seater stadiums. The ones I had been to (Derby, Bolton and Southampton) all failed to inspire and just did not have the same atmosphere as their predecessors. That is one of the main problems: they do not have the soul of the older, less uniform grounds. Is it a coincidence that many clubs with newly built arenas have been relegated since they were built? The big clubs had resisted initially, but Liverpool will soon follow Arsenal in moving to a nearby modern stadium with increased capacity, leaving the place where their history had been built up. Some say Anfield lost something after the old Kop became seated. Will leaving their traditional home take some of the soul or spirit out of the club? I sincerely hope not, but it remains to be seen. I think it will be terribly sad when Liverpool leave Anfield to move to a purpose built home in Stanley Park. The tradition and history associated with the great club will be lost to some extent. No longer will teams see the sign "This is Anfield" as they enter the pitch – unless they take the sign with them of course, but it would not have the same meaning displayed elsewhere. What a piece of memorabilia that would be if they auctioned it off.

There is regular talk over whether Spurs will have to leave White Hart Lane to increase their capacity; poor local travel infrastructure and the stadium being in a residential area (thus restricting outward expansion) are potential obstacles to staying put. The current Board's preference is apparently to stay at the old stadium and I hope they do everything they can to enable the current ground to have an increased capacity. The new Olympic Stadium in Stratford and the new Wembley have both been touted as alternative possibilities. Neither of these are anywhere near Tottenham. It is clear that we need an increased capacity, but I hope dearly that this can be achieved at White Hart Lane. For me, Spurs away from White Hart Lane just would not be the same. There are only three possible constants in football: the name of the club, the fans (which is why we say "we") and the ground. After all, we are Tottenham, super Tottenham, from the Lane. Not Stratford.

Sadly I fear that within the next decade we may have to move away from the Lane to allow more fans to see the games and give the club a stadium to enable it to compete with the other top sides. It is a saddening thought. If it were to happen, getting to the stadium's final game would be imperative. It might offer a full sense of closure, a little like going on one last date to talk things through at the end of a long-term relationship.

Before the match, we walked a lap of the outside of Anfield, ending at the Hillsborough Memorial, adorned with flowers from both home and away supporters. As we turned to find our entrance to the Anfield Road stand, a Liverpool supporter approached us, shook Stu's hand and wished us good luck. I had never come across this in football before, and it touched the three of us, mainly because of the animosity you usually encounter from opposition fans. I wish there was more of this kind of behaviour in football, but if I ask myself if I would approach an opposition fan in a similar manner, I would have to admit I would not for fear of a negative reaction, but also because I could not wish another team luck; I am not gracious enough to mean it. This one Liverpool supporter added something to the day.

After the minute's silence for the Hillsborough Disaster had been impeccably observed by both sets of fans, the game itself was as exciting an encounter I had seen in a long time, played throughout in a generally friendly atmosphere. Spurs took the lead twice in a 2-2 draw, the first time through a swerving thunderbolt from fully 40 yards out from left-back Erik Edman, his first goal for the club, which sent us into raptures. It was without a doubt one of the best goals I have seen live. When Keane put us 2-1 up in the second half it looked for a while as though we might get to be part of history and see a rare Anfield victory. Alas, it was not to be. Both teams played an entertaining passing game, with a mixture of neat one-touch football in midfield and longer balls out to the wings. Liverpool probably felt they deserved the win, and Gerrard missed a penalty, wildly blazing wide. As a Spurs fan, though, I was happy with the result and the truly special matchday occasion.

As the end of the season approached, Spurs were in with a chance of qualifying for Europe through their league position for the first time in 22 years. Seventh place would mean playing in the UEFA Cup next year, a great achievement given the chaotic start to the season and the awful previous campaign. A handful of teams were competing for this place with two weeks of the season remaining. One of these was Aston Villa, and so a win against them at home, however narrow or scrappy, was essential. As it turned out, the victory was an incredibly easy one. Spurs were 3-0 up after 26 minutes, and the first half was dominated by a delightful display of passing football by Tottenham. A couple of days before the match, Martin Jol had called for the fans to be the 12th man. This resulted in a near party atmosphere all through the match, no doubt aided by Tottenham goals spread throughout the 90 minutes. The final score was 5-1, the last goal from right-back Stephen Kelly in the last minute ensuring that we progressed into seventh place on goal difference with just two games to go.

It was a masterful end to the season for me on a personal note but only one point from the remaining two games put any hopes of qualifying for the UEFA Cup firmly to bed. It had been a vastly improved season nonetheless and a final position of ninth slightly disguised the fact that, since Jol took the reigns, for once we had been better than a run-of-the-mill mid-table team.

The 2005/06 season started very optimistically. The previous season's resurgence under Jol and the addition of further players to the squad meant that all Spurs fans believed that we were finally capable of challenging for trophies and European places. In Jol's first full season, surely the target must have been to earn a place in the following season's UEFA Cup, something that was all too rare these days.

My first taste of action that season was against Liverpool. There was a certain buzz around the ground before and during the game. The best starting eleven to represent Spurs for years took to the pitch that day. We had a string of talented players on show, many of whom were current England internationals; they included Paul Robinson in goal, Ledley King as captain in defence, an exciting midfield of Aaron Lennon, Michael Carrick, Jermaine Jenas and Edgar Davids, while Jermain Defoe was up front. We also had Robbie Keane on the bench. Everybody finally believed in the team and was enjoying the day. Although the game finished 0-0, it was a positive afternoon. We matched one of the best teams in the country and for the final quarter of the game you could sense Liverpool were content to settle for a draw, something the big teams would never have done in recent years at White Hart Lane.

Rather strangely, both teams had a headed goal direct from a corner disallowed because the ball had gone out of play during its flight into the penalty area. I left the stadium in an upbeat mood after the game, proud to be a Spurs fan and convinced we were finally, after years of mediocrity, going to be a force in the Premiership. I was looking forward to the rest of the season.

On the Friday morning before the north London derby the weekend was all set up to be one of pure happiness. I was due to find out the long-awaited results of my assessments for a top graduate career programme that would have seen me moving back to working in London. I felt the assessments had gone well and if successful my career would have been well established.

Then there was the big derby game against Arsenal on the Saturday and it looked as though Spurs had their best chance in years of winning. We were third in the league and looking like a very good team. Arsenal on the other hand were lying eighth in the table and had not won away all season in the Premiership. They also had injuries to a couple of key players, including their talisman Thierry Henry. For once Tottenham were favourites to beat their north London rivals. The last time I had seen us beat Arsenal was in November 1995, almost a full decade previously.

My perfect weekend was ruined somewhat on the Friday afternoon. I received email notification that I had been unsuccessful in my job application, despite my thoughts that I had done well. To be honest I had expected their answer to be the opposite of what it was. I felt shocked, disgruntled and wondered what I would do next. I had been pinning a lot on it. After the initial thoughts of doom, gloom and devastation I realised this could still be a good weekend in a different way. I was now thinking of shifting my career to something entirely new. A new dawn you might say, the same thing I hoped to be witnessing on Saturday too.

The atmosphere inside White Hart Lane was again one of real optimism before the game. The fans were convinced we would win. We were sat in the East Stand upper tier, the only part of the ground I had never sat in before. The noise from even this, a traditionally quieter part of the stadium, was at times deafening. As Paul Robinson, our goalkeeper, took his position before kick off he was greeted with "England's number one" ringing in his ears from all sides of the ground. It was quite an uplifting sight and sound. In his short time at the club he had quickly become a firm fans' favourite.

Spurs came storming out of the blocks and dominated the first half. They were passing and playing with flair and excitement, pressing Arsenal into mistakes. On 17 minutes Ledley King met a free kick six yards out and powered it under the body of the Arsenal goalkeeper Jens Lehmann. The stadium erupted. This was it; we were outplaying Arsenal and looked like running out easy winners. I was ecstatic and my troubles of the previous day were, momentarily at least, put to the back of my mind. A few minutes after the goal a beautiful passing movement set up Michael Carrick 25 yards from goal. He hit a screamer a foot wide of the post. If that had hit the back of the net, there would have been bedlam inside White Hart Lane. Carrick was the pick of the players in that first half, running the midfield with a mixture of simple and probing passing. As well as his effort on goal, Spurs had several others and should have gone in two or three goals up at half time. As it was we had to settle for a slender one goal advantage.

The single goal did not turn out to be enough and the match turned out to be the epitome of a game of two halves. Tottenham's relentless effort in the first half meant that the team ran out of steam fifteen minutes into the second half. This, combined with a much improved display of passing and movement from Arsenal, resulted in them having the better of the second period. Despite their increasing pressure on goal, their equaliser actually came after an uncharacteristic goalkeeping error by Robinson, which allowed Pires to pass the ball into an empty net. The game ended 1-1. Not quite a new dawn, but Spurs were now competing on the same level as the top teams; they had also come back from a goal down to get a draw away at Manchester United on the previous Saturday. The result did mean, however, that when I next attended a north London derby, over a decade would have passed since I last saw us beat Arsenal. Not a pleasant statistic but it will just make it all the sweeter when we do triumph again.

Tottenham's good form in the Arsenal game, although maybe not fully matched subsequently, continued over the next couple of months until Christmas. It resulted in us achieving fourth place in the table following a 3-2 victory over Sunderland on 3rd December. A further bonus was the fact that we were also still above Arsenal. Spurs were playing well, scoring goals and, crucially, had turned White Hart Lane into a fortress; unsurprisingly, Chelsea had been the only team to beat us (twice) on home soil in 2005.

As the new year dawned, Spurs still sat in that fourth place. If they stayed there, the Champions League beckoned next season. As is usual, the third round of the FA Cup was staged on the first weekend in January. At the time, the final was due to be the first at the new Wembley (as it later turned out the many cynics were correct in their predictions and the stadium was nowhere near finished in time). Tottenham's cup tradition, coupled with the current form, meant the superstitious among us thought the Cup could well make the short journey from Wembley to the Lane in May.

Unfortunately, the players clearly did not have the same belief, squandering a 2-0 lead away at Leicester to lose 3-2 in the last minute. I was watching on television. It was heart breaking. Following the exit to Grimsby at the first hurdle of the League Cup, Spurs had gone out of both cup competitions at the first stage for the first time since the 1974/75 season.

There were still Champions League aspirations, however, and the club could now concentrate fully on achieving this. Nevertheless, the cup exit seemed to have a hangover effect on the players. Spurs had very winnable matches through January and February, but managed to put together a run of one win in six.

At the end of January, James was fortunate enough to get us complimentary tickets for the evening fixture at Fulham. The only downside was that we were to be sat with the home supporters. James, Stu and myself met after work for a few beers on Fulham High Street, a much more salubrious area of London than the run-down and dirty Tottenham. We were not overly worried about sitting with the Fulham fans, who have a reputation as some of the friendliest and least boisterous in the division.

Our luck ran out as we found ourselves in the back row of Fulham's main support stand, surrounded by about the only twenty or so fans who sang and chanted. Great. We had hoped to blend into the otherwise sedate crowd and be inconspicuous throughout. It is a difficult skill to sit and watch your team with supporters of the opposite team, in their stand. You really have to try hard not to bleat out shouts of joy or frustration and not to clap at the wrong time. I am sure the fans next to us knew we were not Fulham supporters, one of the loudest of whom took great pleasure from banging the metal railings right behind my head on several occasions to aid the noise volume for some of their chants.

The game itself was terrible, neither side, especially Spurs, seemingly capable of taking control of the match. Tottenham's unfortunate striker, Grzegorz Rasiak, a short term fix who left the club a few days after this game, was described as "marginally better than playing with ten men" by Sky Sports and simply as "desperate" by the Guardian.

About half way through the second half, Spurs had their centre-back Michael Dawson sent off for a second yellow card. This seemed to urge the remaining players into action and for the last twenty minutes or so Tottenham looked most likely to win the match.

Nevertheless, the game was deserving of a 0-0 draw. This would have been a fair result, too. Then, in the 92nd minute, Fulham won a free kick, which was delivered straight on to the head of one of their unmarked players six yards out. The ball sailed beyond the dive of Robinson and into the net. As the Fulham fans jumped about around us, we headed straight for the exit, not wanting to be surrounded by people wildly celebrating a last minute Tottenham loss. Many Fulham supporters seemed to follow us, apparently happy that their team had won, but not wanting to celebrate the moment. I did not understand that. Their team, who were on the fringes of a relegation scrap, had just scored a last minute winner against one of the current top four. Getting home was more of a concern for them than basking in the win.

The game typified the run Spurs were on. Several bad results and late goals conceded meant we were unable to pull away from the chasing pack and cement ourselves in fourth place.

The battle for that final spot in Europe's premier competition was taking on a similar appearance to the previous season when Merseyside rivals Everton and Liverpool were both reluctant to put a string of results together and claim fourth place as their own. Just as Spurs were beginning to falter, the nearest rivals, notably Arsenal, started dropping points too. I was just hoping Spurs would do what Everton ended up doing by clinging on as their local neighbours demonstrated an inability to win games they really should have.

Of course, Liverpool made up for not finishing in the top four by actually winning the Champions League trophy itself. UEFA had apparently never considered it possible for a team finishing outside the competition's qualifying places in their own league to win the trophy in the same season. England are currently allocated four places in the Champions League each season, and UEFA had to make the decision whether to disappoint the team who had rightly qualified through their league position or the holders of the trophy. Both clubs were understandably adamant that they should be allowed to compete and Europe's governing body took the easy decision and granted them both a place in the following season's competition.

With the benefit of hindsight, UEFA were now aware that a team could simultaneously win the Champions League and not qualify through a high league position. Just for Tottenham's benefit, it seemed, they decided that if the same thing happened again the Champions League winners would take the qualifying place that the team finishing fourth had worked so hard for nine months to achieve. Unfortunately, Arsenal were still in the Champions League and looking good.

Spurs went into the game at home to Blackburn on the first weekend in March still occupying fourth place. Blackburn were one of the handful of teams now snapping at Tottenham's heels, and the game had taken on the status of a must-win six-pointer.

There was a good atmosphere before the game, the fans sensing the importance of the next 90 minutes. The players seemed to sense it also and started the game well. The team had appeared nervous over recent weeks and I commented beforehand how an early goal would be ideal. To my delight it duly arrived, and in spectacular fashion.

We were sat about ten rows back directly behind the goal at the Park Lane end. A throw-in next to the goal line was directed towards a Robbie Keane run. In one swift movement, without the ball bouncing, he flicked it over his marker's head, rounded another defender and drilled home from five yards out. This all happened a matter of metres from where we were sat. It was a moment of sublime skill, all executed with incredible speed and precision.

Spurs remained on top for the majority of the first half, Keane poaching a second slightly fortuitously. A couple of minutes later, as we were still discussing our second goal, Blackburn broke down the right and a cross from their Welsh striker Craig Bellamy found the diving head of Sinama-Pongolle.

Going in at half time 2-1 up was not the end of the world as long as we came out and played in the second half as we had in the first. Blackburn, however, came out of the blocks running and for half an hour hammered our defence. We could not keep hold of the ball; each time we gained possession we gave it straight back to them to mount another attack.

Their equaliser was inevitable, the only surprise being how long it took before our defence finally gave way. About five minutes before their equalising goal, a Blackburn long range shot headed straight towards us behind the goal, the top corner of the net the only thing standing in its way. Just as I feared the net would bulge, Robinson sprung to his left and somehow palmed the ball over the bar. Sitting so close to such skill carried out at such speed, as with the Keane goal, was quite phenomenal. It makes you realise just how good the top professional players are.

The way the second half was bearing out, Blackburn looked likely winners. However, just as they had scored straight after our second, we did after theirs. Aaron Lennon, our tiny, nippy winger who had broken into the team and performed to such a standard that he was eventually included in the England World Cup squad that summer, broke down the right almost immediately from the kick off and crossed to the Egyptian striker Mido, who did his best to miss from two yards out. Luckily the ball crept under the bar, hitting the roof of the net. Cue pandemonium in the stands. Feelings of despair at giving away a two goal lead were displaced with euphoria and no little relief.

The game really opened up after that, and both teams had several chances. From the point of view of a neutral spectator it really was a cracking game, flowing from end to end with no lack of passion from either side. The last few moments were nervous ones for me though. This would be such an important victory, enabling us to maintain our lead over Arsenal and our other challengers; it was all the more important with a likely defeat away at Chelsea to come the following Saturday. The fans were trying to get behind the players to edge them over the finish line.

Amid a barrage of whistles from the crowd, the referee blew the full time whistle and "Glory, Glory Tottenham Hotspur" broke out around the Lane. As the evening grew dark, I looked to the skies and joined in with a meaningful chorus of "Are you watching, Arsenal?"

The following Saturday, my Chelsea supporting friend Rosie, an old housemate from Sheffield, kindly took me to Stamford Bridge using a spare family season ticket. It felt like I was almost a regular match-goer again, going to consecutive matches.

I was not expecting anything from the game but a loss. A mixture of the lunchtime kick off and South West Trains meant I missed the first twenty minutes. A train from Winchester was already 25 minutes delayed when they announced it was so late it had to terminate at Woking instead of continuing into London. This of course made everyone even later than they already were.

When I finally arrived at Fulham Broadway tube station, I scurried along the Fulham Road to avoid missing as much of the game as possible. As I approached the stadium I heard the unmistakable roar that signalled a goal for the home side. The noise was too loud to be an away goal. My fears were confirmed as I took my seat, the scoreboard reading 1-0 to Chelsea. On the positive side, at least that was one Chelsea goal I would not have to pretend to be happy about.

My seat was high in the East Stand, right on the half way line, which gave a superb view of the match, one I was not used to; it was interesting to see how the game developed and the movement the players made. It also meant I was not surrounded by the hardcore Chelsea support, as I had terrifyingly been on a couple of previous occasions as a teenager.

Rosie informed me that I had, in fact, missed a Spurs-dominated first quarter. After that, however, I witnessed mainly Chelsea pressure. It came as some surprise, therefore, that Spurs scored right on the stroke of half time. It was a slightly surreal moment as the ball crept into the far corner of the net courtesy of England midfielder Jermaine Jenas. I had not been expecting it and had no planned strategy for how to react in a situation where I would normally be jumping for joy. As I watched the Spurs fans celebrating behind the goal, I slowly clenched tight the fist that I was leaning on. I somehow managed to suppress my feelings.

I imagine it is somewhat like tantric sex: trying to control the moment of excitement, until, had Spurs got something from the game, being able to unleash the explosion of joy at a later time (probably in a Stamford Bridge toilet I was thinking – the celebrating that is, not the tantric sex).

Unfortunately, it materialised that I did not have to worry about such things. I sat out the second half, in which Spurs matched Chelsea for passing and chances. A point at Stamford Bridge would have been an unexpected bonus and the team had not been disgraced by any stretch of the imagination. As the game crept towards the 90 minute mark, Spurs did what they had often done in recent weeks: conceded a last minute goal. William Gallas, the Chelsea left-back, seized on a ball loosely given away by our defence. He cut inside and drilled a screamer into the top corner beyond the despairing dive of Robinson.

The players, and myself, were devastated. I somehow also had to contend with overjoyed Chelsea fans celebrating around me, and then when the final whistle blew, singing their anthem "Blue is the colour ...". It was like a dagger being twisted inside my stomach and I felt sick. I just had to stand there and concentrate on leaving the stadium. It certainly was a test of my self control.

The result was no more than I had expected but the manner of the defeat was hard to take. Away matches, sitting with the home fans, in south west London, had taken on the same characteristic that season: both losses due to last minute goals. In the case of Chelsea, it was now sixteen years and counting since out last league victory over them.

Spurs were still fourth with four weeks to go after grinding out a couple more wins in late March. We had held that position for over four months now but it still remained to be seen how the team would cope with the finishing straight.

For once Spurs were entering the last few fixtures of a season where each and every match mattered. It made a pleasant change and added to the excitement. The results of your nearest rivals are also vital and you end up supporting their opposition every week almost as much as you support your own team. I think it is for this reason that every football fan loves cup football; every match matters; it is do or die.

There is not always the same importance, though, so why does every match still matter when you are out of the running for things or when it is too early in the campaign to know which results will have an effect on the outcome of the season? The simple answer is that each and every match matters because fans of a football club want to see their team win. But there are also other things that creep into games to give them added importance even when the result will not impact on your season drastically. First, it is simply a matter of goals: you want to see your team score them, either as part of an emphatic victory or as a winner in the last few minutes, even as a lifeline when you are trailing. There is also always that unrealistic hope that one win will cause an upturn in fortunes and spur the team on to win all their remaining games. Also, you always want to win big games against London teams or top opposition for bragging rights and the atmosphere at this type of game is conducive to making things seem more important than they are. Finally, there can be little things specific to a particular game that make it winnable at all costs: an ex-Tottenham player (or manager) on the opposition team, some history from the last time the two teams played, revenge for a cup exit earlier in the season or even things that materialise from incidents during a game, either from the fans or the players. In short, every game matters to a football supporter.

The Manchester City game in April was a Saturday lunchtime kick off and as such had a strangely quiet atmosphere, as though everybody was still waking up. The players, too, seemed quite apathetic for much of the match.

Having said that, Spurs got off to a lively start and should have been a couple of goals up before they actually took the lead. The City team were awful, their defending in the first half sloppy to say the least. Their 'keeper, David James, was up to his comical old tricks and was getting some over-the-top stick from the fans behind the goal. The defence was giving our players, and Robbie Keane in particular, far too much space in the final third of the pitch but initially we were not incisive enough at the crucial moments.

Just as I was fearing our first half dominance would not be rewarded, Keane turned brilliantly on the edge of the box. David James could only parry his shot and Paul Stalteri, the mishap-prone right-back, tapped in from six yards. It was the least we deserved.

Within minutes of the second half getting underway, Michael Carrick added a second, before City pulled a careless goal back. The win never really seemed in doubt though. City were lacklustre and never looked remotely threatening. Their lack of inspiration seemed to rub off on the Spurs players and the second half passed by all too uneventfully.

The fans, myself included, were anxious to hear the final whistle. The win was vital and when confirmed by the referee was greeted with cheers of relief. The performance may not have been inspiring but the win was so so important at this stage of the season.

As always, I awoke early before my last game of the season, which was to be against Manchester United just ten days after seeing us beat their neighbours City. Nervousness had been added to the excitement I usually felt. Results were still going Tottenham's way and we were four points ahead of Arsenal with four games to play. The other contenders had slipped back so it seemed a straight race between us and Arsenal for that fourth spot.

Manchester United's hopes of catching Chelsea and winning the Premiership title were virtually non-existent. Nevertheless, they were still in good form, and Rooney was on top of his game with the World Cup looming. I had no real expectation of winning the game; a draw seemed the best we could hope for. There was, however, always hope and I let my mind wander before the game: how good would it be if we beat United?

Surprisingly, it looked as though it could happen as Spurs came out of the blocks fastest. Defoe should have scored twice in the first five minutes right in front of us. However, it was United who took the early lead, following a swift counter attack. Spurs were not, it seemed, affected by the early setback and kept coming at United and creating chances. The equaliser looked imminent but it was United who scored again before half time following a dreadful mistake from our left-back Young-Pyo Lee. It was a devastating blow.

Soon after the goal, I witnessed something I had not really seen before at Spurs. A section of the crowd decided to boo the Korean defender when he got his next touch. Tottenham fans have gained a reputation for sometimes getting on a player's back if they do something wrong. On this occasion, however, the majority of the crowd jumped to Lee's defence, shouting down the boo-boys. Even more startling was that the next couple of times he touched the ball, he was actively cheered by the supporters. It had been a season of team achievement and it was great to see the majority of fans vocally back the player over the minority of fans sat around them.

We went in at half time 2-0 down, a most bizarre scoreline given the 45 minutes just past. The game had been fantastic, two quality teams playing attractive passing football with quality and verve. It was end to end, fast attacks characterising the game. The atmosphere was superb, suitably reflecting the big game on the pitch. United had a quality team and their travelling supporters are also some of the best in the league. The noise from them and from us was continuous and loud throughout. There was no real animosity, both sets of fans enjoying the game and willing their team to score.

Given the superior first half performance, there still seemed something in the game for Spurs despite the two goal deficit. The players again started the second half positively, pressurising the United defence at every opportunity. The deserved reward arrived only a few minutes after the restart, Jermaine Jenas prodding the ball home from close range. Game on.

Although the match did lull for a period in the second half, the same high tempo and standard was maintained by both teams throughout. Unfortunately, there was to be no second breakthrough for Spurs but the team never gave up. When we won a last minute corner, Paul Robinson raced up the pitch into the United penalty area. The corner came to nothing and Robinson got nowhere near the ball but it would have been a dream equaliser had the goalkeeper scored. I am sure he would have turned to race the full length of the pitch to celebrate with his adoring Park Lane supporters, with whom he has a special rapport. The fans at that end had even sung happy birthday to him before one game, producing a giant banner to accompany their tune. He returned the gesture by buying a load of footballs, pumping them up himself and launching them into the Park Lane stand before one game at Christmas.

The fans appreciated the players' effort and performance, and maintained the enthusiastic level of support for the entire 90 minutes. As the game entered the final few seconds, something extraordinary happened. I had never before been part of three sides of White Hart Lane standing and singing "We love you, Tottenham" through the sounding of the final whistle, not once pausing, even though the game was lost. It continued for a couple of minutes after the game. I am getting goose bumps writing about it now.

Spurs had matched Manchester United that afternoon, which showed how far the team had come in the last year. Michael Dawson, Michael Carrick and Robbie Keane were all outstanding, Keane covering every metre of the pitch from attack to sliding clearances in his own six yard box.

Despite the heroics, the United result meant that Arsenal were catching. They were four points adrift with a game in hand. Spurs only had three games left but Arsenal's run-in was far easier. This scenario meant that five days after the United game, the mother of all north London derbies, away at Highbury, had been set up. Surely, never before had a league derby mattered so much, certainly not in my lifetime.

As sporadic match-goers, tickets for the game were never going to be a possibility. James, Stu and myself met in a pub for the lunchtime kick off. Despite the importance of the match, I had a complete absence of pre-match nerves. This may have had something to do with my tiredness and slight hangover caused by my late night the day before.

As the match progressed, there was no need for any nerves to emerge either as Spurs were dominating all over the pitch. Michael Carrick was running the midfield and almost scored what would have been one of the goals of the season just before half time after running past the Arsenal midfield, defence and goalkeeper before hitting the side netting. The worrying thing was that no matter how one sided the first half was, it was 0-0 at half time. And Arsenal had Thierry Henry ready and waiting on the substitutes' bench.

The second half continued as the first had been, Spurs dominating but unable to find a breakthrough. With half an hour remaining Henry made his entrance onto the pitch. Such is his presence that you could almost feel the Arsenal team and crowd being lifted.

But it was Spurs who responded a couple of minutes later. As they built another attack, two Arsenal players collided in midfield and went down. Spurs retained possession and the referee quickly enquired after the players. Happy that neither was seriously injured and that they were getting to their feet, Spurs and the referee played on. Carrick fed Davids who crossed for Robbie Keane to slide the ball into the net. The Spurs end at Highbury was delirious and slow motion replays of the goal beautifully captured the fans bouncing in supreme joy as Keane stood triumphant in front of them. It mirrored how we were celebrating in front of the pub television, jumping around as we would have in the stadium, completely oblivious to the other patrons.

Arsenal, and their manager Arsene Wenger in particular, were furious, believing that Spurs should have kicked the ball out of play. They were the only ones though, as the referee, commentators, pundits, journalists and neutral fellow commuters on the way to work on the Monday morning all saw nothing wrong with the goal. It was widely acknowledged that Spurs had every right to continue their attack.

Wenger's fuse was lit, Keane's goal acting as the incendiary device. He confronted Martin Jol on the touchline, something that seemed ill advised, not only because of potential repercussions from the FA, but also due to the size and build difference of the two men. While Jol resembles a bear (albeit a friendly one), Wenger looks more like a stick insect, or maybe a stoat at best.

In the post-match interviews, Wenger reprehensibly labelled the goal a disgrace and repeatedly called Jol a liar, as the Tottenham manager had claimed he was watching a different part of the pitch and not the incident in question. He also refused to shake Jol's hand. Any respect I had for Wenger, his tactics and style of play, was somewhat diminished by this petulant and aggressive behaviour. Jol did well not to rise to the bait. Wenger never did apologise, at least not publicly.

It was all irrelevant anyway, as Spurs had scored a perfectly legitimate goal to go into the lead. Unfortunately, the presence of Henry eventually paid off for Arsenal; he scored an equaliser with seven minutes remaining.

I would have taken a draw before the game as it left finishing in fourth place entirely in our hands. The result, however, was tinged with disappointment, having outplayed Arsenal for the majority of the game and, indeed, for the second time that season. Still, two wins at home to Bolton and away to West Ham would ensure a top four finish and a place in the coveted Champions League.

"Benayounnnn!" The radio commentator on BBC Five Live screamed the name of the West Ham midfielder as he put the Hammers 2-1 ahead with ten minutes to go. That was it. All our hopes dashed. To make matters worse Henry had just completed his hatrick. I went to sit on my bed, distraught.

I had not really thought too much about the final game of the season in the days beforehand. My nerves appreciated it. Then on Saturday lunchtime I decided to watch the BBC's Football Focus for the weekend's preview. That was it; I could think of nothing else until the following afternoon when all the matches were kicking off. My general mood was sullen as a result.

Spurs had beaten Bolton in their penultimate game, but Arsenal had won their two games too, which meant that we had to match their result on the last day of the season to finish fourth. It was still in our hands though. It was agonising on the ears as I listened on the radio. Disastrously, Spurs went 1-0 down just as Arsenal took the lead against Wigan. Then Wigan equalised, and soon after went ahead; at that moment Tottenham equalised too. The balance was swinging one way then the other, but as the half time whistles were blown both teams were level with their respective opponents. My nerves were in shreds. The experience was made no better by the fact that I was listening to the commentary with my Arsenal-supporting wife, who was obviously cheering each goal where my head sunk.

Despite my eternal optimism where Spurs are concerned, something deep down told me it was going to be Arsenal's day. It was their last ever match at Highbury and for sentimentality's sake you just knew they would win, which meant we had to win as well. Sure enough, soon after half time, Henry put them ahead, meaning that Spurs needed to get a winner too. We did not seem to be creating any chances, however, as the second half progressed. Time was running out and it was getting desperate.

And then Benayoun and Henry struck, condemning Spurs to a place in the UEFA Cup, when for five months we had occupied the final Champions League qualification place. The fact that we had just given that place to Arsenal made my despair even worse. I was absolutely gutted. Finishing fourth, and the prospect of competing with Europe's elite, would have been the club's finest achievement in my time supporting them. I know we would not have actually won anything but finishing in the top four in an era where the league has been completely dominated by Chelsea, Manchester United, Liverpool and Arsenal would really have been a great success.

The night before the match, several Spurs players went down with what was supposed to be quite severe food poisoning in the team hotel. All sorts of conspiracy theories were flying around. Maybe Arsene Wenger had got a second job as a chef for that weekend and acted in revenge for that Highbury goal. Unlikely. In the end it turned out to be a stomach bug that had passed from one player to many others. Whatever the cause, many Spurs players could not play against West Ham and many others played when they were in no fit state to do so. It meant that for the most important league game in years, Spurs were disadvantaged from the start. It is no use complaining though; we outplayed Arsenal twice that season and did not beat them once. They finished two points above us. If we had managed to turn one of the draws into a victory, the West Ham game would have been academic anyway. We only had ourselves to blame.

The season had still been a very good one. Fifth was the highest finish since the days of Gascoigne and Lineker in 1990. We played some exciting and fluent football, and several players had had phenomenal seasons. In actual fact, I wrote to Jol to tell him this and thank him. Sadly he did not reply, not that I really expected him to. The new recruitment strategy had ensured we had built a team full of young English internationals; in one England friendly during the course of that season there were five Spurs players on the field at one point. The England squad for the 2006 World Cup contained four players (without the injured Ledley King), which was testament to the development at the club over the past couple of years.

The future looked promising. We had to build on this now and progress further but realistically the domestic and UEFA cups still looked like being the only chance of a trophy. Infiltrating the top four would get harder with every year. I had developed great hopes and expectations, well mainly hopes, throughout the season and especially as the second half of the campaign progressed. So despite it being the best season for sixteen years, I felt deflated as all my hopes were dashed on the season's final afternoon. It was back to the feeling of 'well, there's always next year', something that had become all too familiar over the past twenty years.

And that is what supporting Tottenham Hotspur is like. You wait expectantly and hopefully for another new dawn, and just when you think it has finally arrived, the sun sets again all too quickly (invariably in the past starting with a 3-0 home defeat to Coventry or some such team). Spurs are consistently inconsistent, the past season apart, meaning they finish consistently in mid-table. It was great for once to have a season competing at the top, even if it does turn out to be a rare one off. It made life more interesting, as has the scrap of a relegation battle in the past, as opposed to the constant security of tenth place each year.

For years I have dreamt of Tottenham winning the League, and only twice in my supporting life have they had a team capable of getting anywhere close: the 1986/87 and 1989/90 seasons, when they finished third each time. Will Tottenham Hotspur ever win the League again? In the current climate of the dominant forces of Manchester United, Arsenal, Liverpool and now Chelsea, it does not look plausible at all. And yet, I retain the hope that they will, maybe in 30 years' time; who knows? Following Greece's unlikely triumph in Euro 2004, Adidas used their improbable victory to create a new advert, using the slogan 'Impossible is Nothing'. I cling to that concept when I dream of Spurs winning the League. In the meantime, I go to the games, look out for the results and follow the club with great passion, just waiting for the next good bit and the hope of a permanent new dawn.

Epilogue

"2-1 Tottenham, Dawson winner in the 89th minute"

Text message

Sent Tues 31st October 2006

A ny book has to end somewhere and the 2005/06 season, representing twenty seasons of supporting the club and being the most successful and promising campaign for many years, seemed the most appropriate place.

A couple of days ago, however, such a historic event occurred that I thought it worthy of inclusion. Every season I try to go to the Chelsea game in the dwindling vain hope that I will eventually see them win the fixture. I sent the text message above to James a few days before the game as an ideal rather than a prediction. The reality was closer to it than I could have ever really hoped.

Sat near the Chelsea fans, the atmosphere was superb. There was singing throughout and no one in the Park Lane end once sat down.

Chelsea started much the better, their passing and movement causing us problems, while they gave us very little space when we

211

attacked. After 15 minutes, Dutch winger Arjen Robben broke through our attempted offside trap. Just as he was about to pull the trigger, Ledley King, who had made up a phenomenal amount of ground, slid in to take the ball out for a corner with one of the best tackles of the season.

Unfortunately, we failed to clear the resulting corner and Claude Makelele volleyed in spectacularly from 20 yards to give Chelsea the lead. At that point, I was thinking "here we go again", expecting yet another Chelsea victory. Ordinarily after going behind so early on, you think to yourself that there is enough time to come back into it. Not when playing Chelsea though; it was more a case of damage limitation. A few minutes later Drogba thought he had scored Chelsea's second but the referee blew for a foul in the box long before he made contact with his header.

We were still struggling to cope with Chelsea's play when we won a free kick in a wide position. An excellent ball was curled into the box and Dawson rose to flick it on into the far corner of the net to record his first goal for the club. White Hart Lane quite literally erupted as Dawson ran ecstatically to the crowd. Luckily, I had moved into the aisle to celebrate because when I looked round to where my seat was two men from the row behind had fallen down onto the seats in front. James and Stu thought I was buried underneath the pile of bodies until they saw me jubilantly celebrating.

Game on. From that moment, as darkness fell and the floodlights illuminated the play, the match opened up and became a wonderful spectacle. Both teams were attacking constantly, the play flowing from end-to-end. The best thing was that we were matching Chelsea and they were struggling to cope (mainly as a direct result of Jol changing his formation). Just before half time, Robbie Keane should have put us ahead. Lennon crossed perfectly but Keane managed to put his free header over the bar.

It had been an exhilarating half and more was to come in the second. We restarted as we had finished the first half, playing some excellent passing football and opening Chelsea up. Just over five minutes had gone when Keane received the ball on the left touchline. He beat the Chelsea full-back once and ran the ball down the line. The Chelsea player caught up with him but Keane beat him again, this time leaving him bemused and sat on the turf. His cross fell to Lennon just down in front of us. He controlled it first time to cut inside the defender. As we held our breath, he coolly placed his shot into the far corner of the net. It was a truly brilliant piece of quickly-performed skill. There was a surge of joy and adrenalin and true pandemonium in the stands. I could not believe this was happening. I did not know what to do with myself; I was dancing in the aisles, completely overjoyed. I had to stop and stand still for a while to regain my breath; as I tried to start singing, I could not manage it.

The remainder of the match was like the most nerve-racking party ever. While we were constantly singing and cheering at the position we found ourselves in, we had to hold on for 40 minutes. In other words, we had to do what Barcelona had not managed in the Champions League a few days previously. Chelsea were undoubtedly capable of scoring once, if not twice. It would be an amazing feat if we could hold on.

The thing is, we did more than that. We continued to play positively with verve and passion. Both sides had chances and we had two very clear cut opportunities where the goal was gaping.

The clock was moving so slowly, though. Every time I looked, only another minute or two had passed. We were matching them in all areas, but my heart was racing uncontrollably. It cannot have been any good for my health. We could do this.

As the game crept into the last few minutes, every time the ball was cleared from the box or they shot high or wide, it was greeted with relief-filled cheers, almost as loud as if a goal had gone in. Chelsea clocked up several corners. As we reached 90 minutes, four minutes of injury time were announced. Four more minutes of this was agonising. Each time the ball was cleared, I was jumping up and down in jubilation. The singing had reached a crescendo in the last 15 minutes. Fans were standing on all sides of the ground, bouncing up and down in full voice. I sang till my throat hurt. It was only with about two minutes of the added time remaining that I let myself believe we would win.

I am not sure I have been involved in scenes like there were at the final whistle before. There was an explosion of joy and relief, in equal measures. Everyone around me was jumping around and hugging each other. James, Stu and I were jumping up and down, arms round each others' shoulders. I had never celebrated so much at a final whistle at a league game. I was so happy and could not believe that we had finally beaten Chelsea in the league. The people in the hospitality suites just behind where we were sat looked amazed at what they saw. It just meant so much. All those years of going and witnessing defeats and the occasional draw. I had waited for this since August 1987, the last time we had beaten Chelsea at home in the league. That was my second ever game as a Spurs supporter at the age of eight. I wonder how many other fans had been at both games; a fair few I imagine.

It felt even better than that great night when we beat them 5-1 in the League Cup semi final. Not only had we ended our barren league run against them, but this Chelsea team, filled with expensive superstars, was far superior to their 2002 side, and they were the reigning Premiership Champions. It was a totally unexpected result, and we had come from behind to beat them, something that not many teams can say they have done in recent years.

Unfortunately, the days after the match were dominated by Chelsea's moaning and criticisms of the referee. How dare we have the audacity to beat them! I really do not want to talk about that here. It would ruin being able to revel in the win.

As the players celebrated on the pitch, I looked around and all four sides of White Hart Lane were rocking in the floodlit stands. If only you could bottle that atmosphere and bottle that feeling, you would be happy all your days.

It took a while to get out of the jubilant ground and the Park Lane stand was the last to empty. I needed a lie down.

What an afternoon; it was one of those special matches that made being a football supporter entirely worthwhile. At last, we had beaten Chelsea.

...From the Lane...

by

Oliver Wright

Available from

www.lulu.com/content/992059

And via the website

www.fromthelanebook.co.uk

Printed in the United Kingdom
by Lightning Source UK Ltd.
134705UK00001B/343-348/A